THE USBORNE
INTERNET-LINKED
WORLD OF
Shakespeare

Wrytten at LONDON by the authors,
Miftress Anna CLAYBOURNE and Miftress Rebecca TREAYS.

Prefented, according to a cunning arrangement, by the designer,
Miftress Mary CARTWRIGHT.

Corrected and amended of all faults, by the editor,
Miftress Felicity BROOKS, Gentlewoman.

With divers illustrations, set forth with most excellent skill
by David CUZIK, a Gentleman of *Scotland,*
and Cecco MARINIELLO, a Gentleman of *Italy.*

A CATALOGUE of the severall parts contained in this volume:

2	Who was Shakespeare?
4	Shakespeare in Stratford
6	Elizabethan beliefs
8	London life
10	Elizabethan theatre
12	The Globe Theatre
14	Drama in Shakespeare's England
16	The tragedies
18	The great tragedies
20	The Roman tragedies
22	The comedies
24	The problem plays
26	The romances
28	The earlier history plays
30	The later history plays
32	Shakespeare's poems and songs
34	Shakespeare's language
36	Issues in Shakespeare
38	Shakespeare through the ages
40	Acting and directing styles
42	Performing Shakespeare
46	Shakespeare as inspiration
48	Plots of Shakespeare's plays
54	Who's who in the world of Shakespeare
56	Glossary of terms and phrases
57	Glossary of Shakespearean words
58	Glossary of Shakespearean characters
60	Important dates
61	Shakespeare Web sites
62	Index

Wrytten with the gracious aide of these wise counsellors:

Christopher GEELAN, Gentleman, of the fam'd *English Shakespeare Company,*
and Dr Robert BEARMAN, a most Senior Archivist, at the house of Wm. Shakespeare, *Stratford-upon-Avon.*

Later review'd, and referr'd to the fantasticall Engine, commonly call'd *Internet,* by Miftress Mairi MACKINNON

Who was Shakespeare?

William Shakespeare was an English playwright and poet who lived in the late 1500s and early 1600s (around 400 years ago). His plays are now performed all over the world in hundreds of languages, and he is known as one of the greatest writers of all time. The reason his work is so popular is that Shakespeare wrote about human nature and how people behave. That is why, although his words can be hard to understand, his ideas are as relevant now as they were four centuries ago.

A picture of Shakespeare which appears at the front of the first published collection of Shakespeare's works, the First Folio (1623).

Prospero and Ariel, two characters from the romance comedy *The Tempest*.

This is a scene from the comedy *A Midsummer Night's Dream*, one of Shakespeare's most famous plays. It shows the fairies and their queen, Titania, with Bottom, a workman with an ass's head.

Go to **www.usborne-quicklinks.com** for a link to a Web site where you can find an excellent introduction to Shakespeare, his life and works.

Shakespeare's works

At least two of Shakespeare's plays have been lost, but 38 survive. Two of these, *Henry VIII* and *The Two Noble Kinsmen*, were co-written with John Fletcher. The other 36 are divided into comedies, tragedies and histories. Shakespeare also wrote poems, including a series of sonnets (a type of short poem). Nobody knows exactly when each of these works were written. This book includes approximate dates on page 60. Some experts have even said that "Shakespeare's" plays are really the work of other writers, such as Francis Bacon, a philosopher who lived at around the same time. This may be because people cannot believe that Shakespeare, who came from an ordinary background, could have written such great works of literature.

Performing Shakespeare

Whenever a new production of a Shakespeare play is staged, directors, designers and actors think of new interpretations, or ways to understand and present it. Plays can be performed in modern dress, or set in any historical period. Directors sometimes cut or change the text of a play. The same scene can be funny, frightening or exciting, depending on how the stage is set and how the actors say the words. This book shows how theatre companies prepare for Shakespeare productions and looks at some of the ways Shakespeare has been interpreted in the theatre, as well as in films, books and cartoons.

In this scene from the tragedy *Hamlet*, a troupe of actors puts on a play in which a king is murdered by having poison poured into his ear.

This woodcut shows a scene from the Roman tragedy *Julius Caesar* in which Caesar is stabbed to death by his former friend Brutus.

Shakespeare's language

Language changes all the time. The way people spoke 400 years ago was different from the way we speak now, and Shakespeare's language can be hard to understand. He used many old words like *slubber*, *lustihood* and *welkin*, as well as words such as *sad*, *fell* and *marry*, which have different meanings today. Most editions of Shakespeare's works help by providing notes which explain the meanings of words and phrases. The glossary on page 57 of this book explains some of the more unfamiliar words.

Line references

Plays are divided into sections called acts and scenes. When quotations from Shakespeare's plays are used in this book, line references like this show which section they come from.

The play's title is written in *italics*.

Macbeth, II.i.35

The line number is written as a normal number.

The act is written in capital Roman numerals.

The scene is in small Roman numerals.

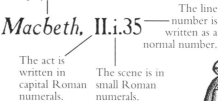

The King rides proudly into battle in the history play *Henry V*.

Shakespeare in Stratford

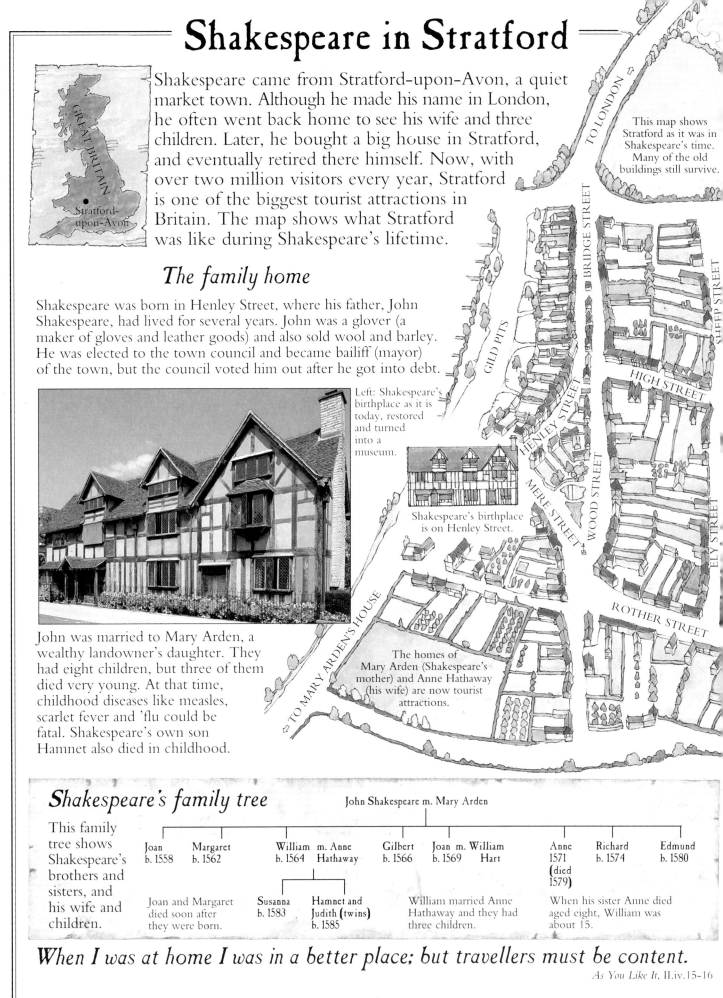

Shakespeare came from Stratford-upon-Avon, a quiet market town. Although he made his name in London, he often went back home to see his wife and three children. Later, he bought a big house in Stratford, and eventually retired there himself. Now, with over two million visitors every year, Stratford is one of the biggest tourist attractions in Britain. The map shows what Stratford was like during Shakespeare's lifetime.

GREAT BRITAIN

Stratford-upon-Avon

This map shows Stratford as it was in Shakespeare's time. Many of the old buildings still survive.

The family home

Shakespeare was born in Henley Street, where his father, John Shakespeare, had lived for several years. John was a glover (a maker of gloves and leather goods) and also sold wool and barley. He was elected to the town council and became bailiff (mayor) of the town, but the council voted him out after he got into debt.

Left: Shakespeare's birthplace as it is today, restored and turned into a museum.

Shakespeare's birthplace is on Henley Street.

John was married to Mary Arden, a wealthy landowner's daughter. They had eight children, but three of them died very young. At that time, childhood diseases like measles, scarlet fever and 'flu could be fatal. Shakespeare's own son Hamnet also died in childhood.

The homes of Mary Arden (Shakespeare's mother) and Anne Hathaway (his wife) are now tourist attractions.

TO LONDON

BRIDGE STREET

SHEEP STREET

GILD PITS

HENLEY STREET

HIGH STREET

MERE STREET

WOOD STREET

ELY STREET

ROTHER STREET

TO MARY ARDEN'S HOUSE

Shakespeare's family tree

This family tree shows Shakespeare's brothers and sisters, and his wife and children.

John Shakespeare m. Mary Arden

| Joan b. 1558 | Margaret b. 1562 | William b. 1564 m. Anne Hathaway | Gilbert b. 1566 | Joan m. William b. 1569 Hart | Anne 1571 (died 1579) | Richard b. 1574 | Edmund b. 1580 |

Joan and Margaret died soon after they were born.

Susanna b. 1583

Hamnet and Judith (twins) b. 1585

William married Anne Hathaway and they had three children.

When his sister Anne died aged eight, William was about 15.

When I was at home I was in a better place; but travellers must be content.

As You Like It, II.iv.15-16

Go to **www.usborne-quicklinks.com** for a link to a Web site that tells you more about the kind of schooling Shakespeare would have had.

Shakespeare's schooldays

Shakespeare went to the King Edward VI Grammar School. Boys usually only went to school if their parents could afford not to send them out to work. (Girls were taught at home, and often didn't learn to read or write.) At school, boys studied mostly Latin. One schoolmaster taught a class of about twelve boys, sometimes with the help of an assistant. Shakespeare left when he was about 15 and started work. He didn't go to a university, but probably read what books he could get hold of in his spare time.

A photograph of the inside of Shakespeare's school, which still stands in Stratford.

The present-day Royal Shakespeare Company has three theatres near the river in Stratford. The company is famous for its Shakespeare productions.

RIVER AVON

WATER SIDE

CHAPEL LANE

New Place, Shakespeare's house in later life.

Hall's Croft, where Susanna Shakespeare lived when she got married.

King Edward VI Grammar School

CHURCH STREET

OLD TOWN

The main church in Stratford is the Holy Trinity Church on the edge of town. Shakespeare was baptized and buried there, and it now contains a monument to him.

Shakespeare's monument in Holy Trinity Church

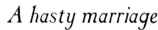

TO ANNE HATHAWAY'S COTTAGE

A hasty marriage

Shakespeare married Anne Hathaway in 1582, when he was 18. She was eight years older than him and pregnant. In those days, as now, it wasn't unusual for women to be pregnant at their wedding. Although sex before marriage was officially a sin, it was usually accepted as long as the mother-to-be got married before the baby was born.

After their first child, Susanna, the couple had twins. So at the age of only 20, Shakespeare had a wife and three children to provide for. His father's business was still in difficulty, and he needed to earn a living. This may have been why he left Stratford for London.

Buying a New Place

Shakespeare bought a large, expensive Stratford house, "New Place", in 1597. This was quite early in his career - he was still working in London most of the time - but it gave his wife and children their own home, and proved to everyone that Shakespeare had paid off all his family's debts. At the end of his career, Shakespeare retired to Stratford and lived at New Place until he died in 1616.

Leaving Stratford

After marrying Anne, Shakespeare probably worked with his father in Stratford, although he might have been a teacher, a lawyer or a soldier. What we do know is that by 1592 he was in London writing plays. He may have left for London with actors who were visiting Stratford with touring theatre companies who could have helped him find a job in the theatre.

Elizabethan beliefs

Life in Elizabethan England could be cruel and hard. The poor often went hungry, disease was widespread, medical remedies often felt more like tortures, and many women died in childbirth. But through their beliefs, people found ways of making sense of their existence.

Just having a tooth pulled out could lead to infection and death.

17th-century medical tools

Religion

People in Elizabethan England were, in general, much more religious than people today. Almost everyone believed in God, and expected to go to heaven or hell after death. In *Hamlet*, Hamlet won't kill his stepfather, Claudius, while Claudius is praying, because he doesn't want him to go to heaven.

At this time, England was a Protestant country – it had broken away from the Catholic Church of Rome. This was part of the European movement called the Reformation, which had started with attacks on corruption in the Catholic Church and led to the founding of non-Catholic, or Protestant, churches.

Edmund Campion, like many other English Catholics, was accused of treason and tortured. He was executed in 1581.

As many wars were fought in the name of religion, all English Catholics were seen as potential traitors to their country and were forbidden to hold any public office.

Some Protestants, called Puritans, felt the Church in England hadn't gone far enough in its rejection of Catholicism. They wanted to "purify" the Church of its remaining Catholic elements, such as bishops and ceremonial robes. Puritans also had strict ideas about what was sinful, or could lead to sin: fine clothes, drinking, gambling and going to see plays were all thought to pave the way to hell.

The Chain of Being

The Chain of Being was a concept the Elizabethans inherited from the Middle Ages. It was an attempt to give order (or "degree" as the Elizabethans often called it) to the vastness of creation. The idea was that God created everything in a strict hierarchy, or chain, that stretched from God himself down to the lowest things in existence. Everything had its own place. Humans occupied a place in the chain below the angels but above animals, plants and stones. Some humans were higher in the chain than others.

The monarch was the highest, with nobles and churchmen below. Then followed gentlemen and finally commoners. All women were considered to be inferior to men, with the obvious exception of Elizabeth I. Her position as monarch outweighed the fact that she was a woman.

Accepting one's place in the chain was a duty that would be rewarded by God in heaven. Disrupting the chain was thought to lead to chaos, but of course many people still did challenge their position in society.

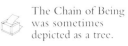

The Chain of Being was sometimes depicted as a tree.

Myths and magic

Fairies, magic, witches, spells and prophecies (utterances that foretell the future) all formed part of the Elizabethan view of life. Folklore and superstition were often as important to people as the official religious beliefs taught by the Church.

In *A Midsummer Night's Dream*, Puck, played here by Toyah Wilcox, is a mischievous fairy.

Many Elizabethans thought that fairies, goblins and sprites came out at night to play tricks on innocent people. It was believed they could make people go insane, give them terrible nightmares or even lure them into a devilish underworld.

This woodcut shows a woman being hanged for witchcraft. She would have been tortured until she "confessed" to being a witch.

Diseases and disasters were often blamed on witches. Many women who didn't fit into society were branded as witches and accused of working for the devil. Astrology – the belief that the position and movement of the stars can foretell and influence events on Earth – was more important than it is today. Respected astrologers could have great influence over people's lives. The astrologer John Dee was said to influence Elizabeth I.

The signs of the zodiac, based on a medieval drawing

Little and large

The human body was thought to be a miniature representation of the universe as a whole. Various parts of the body were linked to the planets and the signs of the zodiac. Things that happened in the universe, which was known as the "macrocosm", were supposed to happen on a much smaller scale within the human body (the "microcosm").

The body was also thought to contain four "humours", or fluids - black bile, phlegm, blood and choler. A person's temperament depended on the way the humours were mixed. In *Julius Caesar*, Mark Anthony describes Brutus as a man in whom all these humours are mixed perfectly. But most people were thought to have one humour that was more dominant than the others.

Illnesses and mental disorders were blamed on an imbalance of the humours. For example, melancholia (depression) was thought to be caused by an excess of black bile.

Hamlet is a famous example of a character with too much "black bile", causing a melancholic (depressive) temperament.

The picture above, based on a sketch in a medieval manuscript, shows the parts of the body and their corresponding zodiac signs.

There are more things in heaven and earth... Than are dreamt of in our philosophy

Hamlet, I.v.168-9

Go to **www.usborne-quicklinks.com** for a link to a Web site where you can read more about the beliefs and superstitions of Shakespeare's day.

London life

By the early 1590s, Shakespeare had arrived in London, England's capital city. It was a thriving port with an expanding population. His first impressions would have been of teeming crowds, the squalor of poverty, and the extravagance of the wealthy. Although none of Shakespeare's plays is set wholly in London, the city must have had a great influence on him. He would have attended lectures on new scientific discoveries, discussed the latest trends in playwriting, listened to tales of foreign lands from merchants and enjoyed the lively night life.

The streets of London were narrow and dirty. This picture shows a typical street opening up into a small marketplace.

In the City, it was against the law to kill large birds such as kites and ravens. They were needed to devour the filth and rubbish in the streets.

A kite

"From Tower to Temple"

A view of London from the south, from an etching by Claes Jan Visscher, made in 1616.

The City of London was said to stretch "from Tower to Temple" – from the Tower of London in the east, to the Temple Bar (the buildings where young men trained to be lawyers) about a mile away in the west. It was bordered to the north by a wall about two miles long, and to the south by the River Thames. Beyond these boundaries were London's suburbs, areas outside the strict control of the City authorities.

This cock-fighting scene was painted in 1615.

In the heart of the City was the great cathedral of St. Paul's. It stood on the same site as the present St. Paul's, which was built after the original was destroyed in the Great Fire of London in 1666. For many Elizabethan Londoners, St. Paul's was more of a general meeting place than a place of worship. Deals were struck, goods were bought and sold, and thieves, prostitutes and beggars operated within its walls. Meanwhile, lessons from the Bible were preached from the pulpits.

There was no shortage of entertainment in London. Apart from the attractions of inns and taverns, cockfighting and bear-baiting were popular sports, and many people enjoyed watching public beatings and executions.

This farmer has come to London to sell bales of wool.

Sewage and waste were poured into open drains.

A raven

Go to **www.usborne-quicklinks.com** for a link to a Web site where you can find out more about life in Elizabethan London.

A beggar

A parish church

London life was punctuated by the sound of church bells. Ninety-seven parish (local) churches stood within the City.

Most buildings had tiled roofs and were made of wooden frames filled with plaster.

Two men being held in pillory as a punishment.

Inns were dens of gambling, thieving and brawling.

A pie seller

A pickpocket

Market stalls

Plague

Crowded conditions and poor sanitation made London an ideal breeding ground for plague, a fatal disease carried by fleas on rats. In 1592-4, 1603-4 and 1623 London was devastated by the disease. Over 100,000 people died.

In this engraving, plague is depicted as a skeleton dancing on coffins, with London in the background.

Artisans (skilled craftsmen) and shopkeepers hung painted signs from their buildings.

Two apprentices having a fight

Elizabethan theatre

A self-portrait by Richard Burbage, one of the biggest stars of the Elizabethan stage.

Until the mid-16th century, most plays were performed outside London. Craftsmen or tradespeople put on traditional plays in town squares and on village greens. As it grew in size and importance, though, London became the centre of English theatre. In Shakespeare's lifetime, theatre became hugely popular. At first it was not considered a very respectable pastime, and most of the theatres were in the rougher parts of town.

A modern British stamp showing the Rose, one of Elizabethan London's theatres.

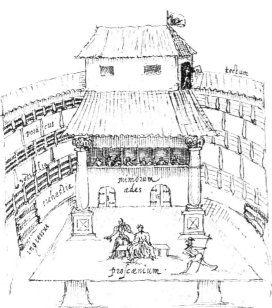

London's theatres

The first London theatre was called The Theatre. It was built in 1576 in north London, just outside the City walls. In 1587, the Rose Theatre was built south of the Thames, among the prisons and brothels of an area called Bankside. The Rose flourished and drew large crowds. In 1595, the huge Swan Theatre, said to hold up to 3,000 people, was built just a few yards to the west. All these theatres were deliberately built outside the City limits, so they were free from the restrictions of City regulations.

As an aspiring dramatist, Shakespeare could not have been in London at a better time. Not only were people flocking to see plays at the theatre, but Queen Elizabeth I loved the theatre and often held performances of plays at her court.

Left: A drawing of the inside of the Swan Theatre, based on a sketch by Johannes de Witt, a tourist from the Netherlands, who visited London in about 1596.

In *A Midsummer Night's Dream*, a troupe of amateur actors puts on a play. Their bad performance is made into a joke by Shakespeare, who belonged to a professional company.

Theatre companies

In London, plays were put on by theatre companies (groups of professional actors). By law, a company had to have a patron, a rich friend who would support it financially. Theatre companies were named after their patrons. For example, the company supported by the Earl of Leicester was called Leicester's Men. Shakespeare spent much of his career with a company called the Chamberlain's Men. Its patron was the Lord Chamberlain. As well as performing in theatres, the company gave private shows for students, noblemen and even the Queen.

In 1603, James I became king. He wanted to be a patron, and started supporting the Chamberlain's Men. From then on, they were known as the King's Men.

Go to www.usborne-quicklinks.com for a link to a Web site where you can find out more about public theatres in Shakespeare's time.

The audience

Theatre in Elizabethan London was an entertainment for everyone, a bit like the cinema today. The cheapest tickets cost one penny, which most ordinary people could afford. (Workers earned a basic wage of about 12 pence a week.) The most expensive tickets were sixpence and were bought by rich merchants and nobles. Foreign traders and tourists often made a trip to the theatre as part of their visit to London. With so many people crowded together, the theatres were also popular with thieves and pickpockets.

Audiences were not as well-behaved as they are today. People jeered at the actors and shouted out rude remarks. Some even climbed onto the stage and joined in with swordfights. People also brought food with them to eat during the performance, or to throw at bad actors.

Stagecraft

Special effects and scenery did not play a big part in Elizabethan theatre. Musicians provided sound effects with drums and trumpets, and the actors often wore extravagant, showy costumes. But audiences were expected to use their imaginations for different locations and backgrounds. This speech from *Henry V* asks the audience to imagine huge battlefields and armies, as they cannot be reproduced on stage:

Can this cock-pit hold
The vasty fields of France? Or can we cram
Within this wooden O the very casques
That did affright the air at Agincourt?
O pardon: since a crooked figure may
Attest in little place a million,
And let us, ciphers to this great account,
On your imaginary forces work. *Henry V*, Prologue,11-18

Theatrical costumes

Plague and players

Theatres were closed during severe outbreaks of plague, because it was feared that the disease spread more quickly in crowds. Many companies left London for tours of the countryside. Players often had to sell their costumes and scripts in order to survive. Some Puritans, who thought theatre-going was a sin, believed that plague was sent by God as a punishment for such wickedness.

Shakespeare's players

Shakespeare is thought to have joined the theatre as an actor, or "player", and become a writer later. It was normal for actors to help write plays, or to change them a lot during rehearsals. Shakespeare probably started gradually writing more and acting less. Actors often specialized in one type of part. Stars like Richard Burbage and William Sly got the big parts, such as leading roles in tragedies. Comic actors or clowns, such as Will Kempe, played a fool or a comic character. There were no actresses. Women's roles were played by boys. Women did not act on stage until the Restoration, after the English Civil War.

This photograph shows Viola, the heroine of the comedy *Twelfth Night*, disguised as Cesario, a pageboy. In Elizabethan times, boys would have played women playing boys.

A woodcut of Will Kempe, who acted with the Chamberlain's Men until 1599.

All the world's a stage... *As You Like It*, II.vii.139-40

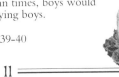

The Globe Theatre

From 1599 onwards, Shakespeare's plays were usually performed at the Globe, a huge, open-air circular theatre in Southwark in London. The theatre could hold 3,000 people, and there were two performances a day. Along with other members of his theatre company, the Chamberlain's Men, Shakespeare owned a share in the Globe and made a lot of money from it.

A flag was flown during a performance.

Like many theatres at the time, the Globe was a wooden circle, with no roof over the middle. The only lighting was daylight, so performances were put on in the afternoons.

Thatched roof

The stage, known as an apron stage, stuck out into the middle of the yard. It was covered by a roof which helped to keep the players dry.

The ceiling over the stage was called the "shadow" or "heavens". It was painted with sun, moon and stars.

Behind the stage there was a backstage area where the actors got changed.

The stage was positioned so the sun didn't shine in the actors' eyes.

The Globe was built of oak beams.

The two wooden pillars supporting the roof were painted to look like marble.

There was not much scenery on the stage. Props and elaborate costumes were used instead.

The stage was 1.5m (5ft) high, so people couldn't jump onto it.

The members of the audience who stood in the yard around the stage were known as groundlings. They weren't sheltered from the rain, but they were nearest to the action on the stage.

There were three levels of covered galleries around the yard. It cost more to sit here and an extra penny if you wanted a cushion.

The Globe needed brick foundations because it was built on marshy ground.

The cloud-capped towers, the gorgeous palaces,
The solemn temples, the great globe itself... *The Tempest*, IV.i.153

Go to **www.usborne-quicklinks.com** for links to two Web sites with information about the original Globe and the new Globe theatres.

The first two Globes

The Chamberlain's Men originally used a theatre called The Theatre, in north London. But they fell out with the landlord, and in 1599 The Theatre was dismantled and its timbers were moved and used to build the Globe. In 1613, a spark from a cannon fired during a performance of *Henry VIII* set fire to the thatched roof, and the Globe burned down. (No one was badly hurt.) It was rebuilt with a tiled roof, and stood until 1644, when the Puritans tore it down during the Civil War.

Part of a 17th-century view of London, showing the Globe Theatre.

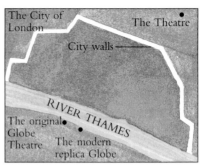

This map of 16th-century London shows the sites of The Theatre and the Globe Theatre, as well as the site of the modern replica of the Globe which was opened in in 1996 (see below).

Global language

Shakespeare sometimes refers to the Globe Theatre in his works. In *The Tempest*, Prospero speaks of "the great globe itself", and in *Henry V*, the theatre is called the "wooden O".

Shakespeare's writing sometimes may reflect the design of the theatre. Some of the lines in his plays have three parts, or a word repeated three times. At the Globe, lines like these allowed an actor to address the audience on all three sides of the stage, which stuck out into the middle of the yard (see picture).

In the first Globe Theatre, the roof was thatched, making it very vulnerable to fire.

"Gatherers" stood at the door with boxes to collect admission money. This is why a ticket office is called a "box office".

Rebuilding the Globe

The new Globe Theatre under construction in London.

In 1970, the American actor Sam Wanamaker started a project to rebuild Shakespeare's Globe Theatre near to its original site in London. Now the Globe has been completed. It is an accurate replica of the first one and is built of the same materials – brick, oak wood, thatch, animal hair and putty. It is used for performances of Shakespeare's plays. Safety regulations mean it can hold only half as many people as the original Globe, but it is still one of London's biggest theatres.

Drama in Shakespeare's England

Ben Jonson (1572-1637), one of the greatest playwrights of Shakespeare's era.

During Shakespeare's lifetime, drama developed faster than ever before. In London, playgoing became a large-scale business. With some theatres holding two or three thousand people, there were huge profits to be made, and new material was always needed. Drama was not seen as "literature", but merely as popular entertainment, in the same way as Hollywood films or television sitcoms and soap operas are now.

A scene from the famous play *Volpone* by Ben Jonson.

Dramatic developments

When Shakespeare was young, he could have watched, or even taken part in, several different kinds of drama. Some towns still followed the medieval tradition of putting on a series of "mystery plays" every summer. These told Bible stories and were performed by the townspeople. Plays were also performed by schoolboys and university students. These plays were often in Latin.

There were also touring companies of actors who visited towns and staged morality plays, dealing with human sin and virtue. They also put on other entertainments such as juggling shows.

The major growth of theatre in London probably began in the late 1580s. The first purpose-built theatre had opened there in 1576. *Tamburlaine* (1587) by Christopher Marlowe (1564-1593) was typical of the new style of drama, telling the story of a powerful conqueror, and *The Spanish Tragedy* (c.1588) by Thomas Kyd (1558-1594) started a trend for revenge tragedies. At this time, a few individual actors became very famous, like film stars today. For example, Edward Alleyn was so popular as Tamburlaine that Marlowe wrote a sequel for him.

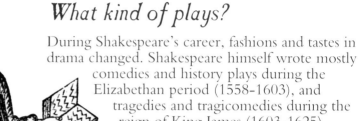

Faustus, from the title page of an edition of *Dr Faustus* by Christopher Marlowe.

What kind of plays?

During Shakespeare's career, fashions and tastes in drama changed. Shakespeare himself wrote mostly comedies and history plays during the Elizabethan period (1558-1603), and tragedies and tragicomedies during the reign of King James (1603-1625).

Tragedy ends in the death of one or more of the main characters. In a revenge tragedy such as *Titus Andronicus*, one murder sets off a chain of revenge killings. Most of Shakespeare's tragedies involve historical individuals and events.

Comedy usually has a happy ending, and can also include jokes, farce and innuendo. Shakespeare's comedies are usually love stories, set far away from England.

Tragicomedy is a mixture of comedy and tragedy. The play seems to move towards a tragic ending, but a twist in the plot saves the characters. Shakespeare's romance plays (see page 26), such as *The Winter's Tale*, are examples of tragicomedy.

Satirical comedies, such as *The Alchemist* by Ben Jonson (1572-1637), attack ideas or individuals by laughing at them. They are similar to comedies, but have a more cynical tone.

History plays usually tell the stories of great leaders and kings. In his history plays, Shakespeare sometimes altered what he found in the history books to suit his own dramatic purposes and make the plays more exciting.

Juliet Stevenson in *The Duchess of Malfi*, a tragedy by John Webster. Most of the characters in this play die in a gory bloodbath.

*The actors are at hand, and by their show
You shall know all that you are like to know*

A Midsummer Night's Dream, V.i.116-117

Go to **www.usborne-quicklinks.com** for a link to a Web site where you can read about other famous playwrights of Shakespeare's day.

Plays, plots and poetry

Although there was a great variety of Elizabethan and Jacobean drama, most playwrights followed a few basic methods, or conventions. Playwrights didn't often make up new plots: they used traditional tales or borrowed ideas from other books. Shakespeare often took two old stories and combined them to make a new one, as in *The Merchant of Venice* (see page 25). Many plays were set in other countries and in times gone by.

Alan Howard as Macbeth. The panic in his face is emphasized by the loosely structured blank verse he speaks (see below).

Plays were written in poetry or prose, or a mixture of both. Playwrights mainly used a kind of unrhymed poetry called blank verse. This uses a type of verse line called an iambic pentameter, made up of five units called iambic feet. An iambic foot has two syllables, an unstressed one followed by a stressed one.

This line from *Macbeth* is a perfect iambic pentameter. The marks show the stressed syllables.

So fair and foul a day I have not seen

Macbeth, I.iii.36

One iambic foot

Shakespeare often broke the rules and wrote lines with a slightly different pattern of stresses. This varied the speeches so that they didn't sound boring. The lines below have varied stresses, which brings them closer to real speech. Try saying them out loud.

Is this a dagger which I see before me,
The handle towards my hand? Come, let me clutch thee.

Macbeth, II.i.33-4

The changing texts

Shakespeare's plays were written to be performed, not printed as books. When they were printed, they weren't always exactly the same as the original version. These are the different stages between Shakespeare's handwritten manuscripts and the texts we have today.

Foul papers

Writers' original manuscripts are called "foul papers" because they contain crossings-out and can be hard to read. None of Shakespeare's foul papers has survived, but three pages of a play called *Sir Thomas More*, written jointly by several authors, are thought to be in his handwriting.

A scribe

Fair copies

A specially employed scribe wrote out "fair copies" for rehearsals. The text often got changed by the actors during rehearsals.

Quartos

Eighteen of Shakespeare's plays were printed as small books, or quartos, while he was alive, but he probably didn't check them. Some quartos were based on what actors could remember of their lines.

Title page from a quarto of *King Lear*.

The First Folio

36 of the plays were collected and published in 1623, in a book now called the First Folio. Shakespeare had died seven years earlier, so he couldn't check the text.

A page from the First Folio

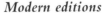

Printers

16th and 17th century printers did their typesetting by hand. They often made mistakes, and sometimes even changed the text to make it fit on the pages.

A 16th-century printing press

Modern editions

Most modern editions are based on the First Folio. But experts still argue over what exactly Shakespeare wrote, and they sometimes try to change passages in the text to what they might have been originally.

15

The tragedies

The tragedies

This is a guide to the approximate dates when the tragedies were written:

Titus Andronicus 1592-3
Romeo & Juliet 1595-6
Julius Caesar 1599-1600
Hamlet 1600-01
Othello 1602-03
King Lear 1604-05
Macbeth 1605-06
Timon of Athens 1606-07
Antony & Cleopatra 1606-07
Coriolanus 1607-08

A tragedy or not a tragedy?

Experts don't always agree on how to divide Shakespeare's plays into categories. Some of the plays are sometimes classed as tragedies and sometimes not. For example, *Timon of Athens*, a story of a generous man who goes insane when his friends desert him, is usually called a tragedy, but some experts think it is more like a satirical comedy. *Cymbeline* and *Troilus and Cressida* are now usually classed as comedies, but they used to be referred to as tragedies in some books.

Shakespeare's tragedies are his most famous and popular plays. They contain his best known characters, such as Romeo and Juliet, Macbeth, Othello and Hamlet, and his most famous quotations. About ten of Shakespeare's plays are usually thought of as tragedies – though many of his other plays, such as the history plays and the problem plays, also have tragic elements.

Solo speeches

In the tragedies, characters often make speeches when by themselves, called soliloquies. For example, in Hamlet's famous speech beginning "To be, or not to be...", Hamlet thinks about whether he should commit suicide instead of trying to kill his uncle, who has murdered his father. Soliloquies can help the audience to understand the main character. They often also emphasize his loneliness.

Tragic heroes

All of Shakespeare's tragedies have a tragic hero, or "protagonist". He is often a man of high rank, such as a king or prince. The protagonist creates, or is put into, a difficult situation which he must try to resolve. But a combination of bad luck and bad decisions lead to his death. For example, Othello is tricked into thinking his wife is unfaithful, and kills her. When he finds she was innocent, he kills himself. He is a victim of an unlucky situation, but also of his own failings. The protagonist is often a relatively sympathetic figure. His soliloquies (see above) show his feelings and motives, and show the audience how easy it would be to make similar mistakes. The pictures below show how one protagonist, Macbeth, makes the wrong decisions, with tragic results...

Tragic heroes are often lonely, intense figures. This cartoon by Narman caricatures the actor John Barrymore playing Hamlet in 1925.

Macbeth, the Thane (Lord) of Glamis, is very ambitious. He does well in battle, but he would like more power...

He meets three witches who predict that he will be king. He realises that if he kills King Duncan, he might rule in his place.

Macbeth's wife would like him to be king too. She puts pressure on him to kill Duncan, and accuses him of being cowardly.

Duncan decides to visit Macbeth at his castle. This gives Macbeth an easy opportunity, and his wife encourages him...

The pressure is too much. Macbeth plucks up his courage and kills Duncan. He regrets it at once, but by then it is too late...

Go to **www.usborne-quicklinks.com** for a link to a Web site where you'll find an online guide to *Romeo and Juliet*, including the famous balcony scene.

Early tragedies: blood, guts and passion

Titus Andronicus and *Romeo and Juliet* are Shakespeare's first two tragedies, written while he was still a young man. *Romeo and Juliet* is set in Italy, and is a love story with many comic elements. Instead of helping to bring about their own downfall, like some of Shakespeare's later tragic heroes, Romeo and Juliet are innocent victims of a terrible mix-up. This sort of plot device is more often used in comedies. In later tragedies, characters are more responsible for their fates.

Left: in *Titus Andronicus*, a sacrifice starts off a chain of increasingly gory revenges between Titus, a Roman general, and Tamora, queen of the Goths. In this picture, Titus's daughter Lavinia has had her hands and tongue cut off by Tamora's sons.

Titus Andronicus is a revenge tragedy, a form which was very popular in Shakespeare's time. The formula for this kind of tragedy was borrowed from ancient Roman tradition. In the play, Titus, a Roman general, and Tamora, queen of a tribe called the Goths, are deadly enemies who launch a series of horrific attacks on each other's families. Titus has his hand cut off, his daughter Lavinia is raped and loses her hands and tongue, and eventually Titus kills Tamora's sons, cooks them in a pie and serves it up to their mother as a revenge. The play is horrific, but shows very vividly how savagely humans can behave when they are hurt and want revenge.

In *Romeo and Juliet*, two teenagers are in love, but their families, the Capulets and the Montagues, are enemies. Here, Romeo visits Juliet in the famous balcony scene.

Doom and destiny

In Shakespeare's time, just as today, many people believed in fate, or destiny, and in the power of the stars to foretell the future. Shakespeare uses the idea of fate or destiny to add excitement and anticipation to the tragedies. For example, he uses prophecy as a way of holding the audience's interest, because everyone wants to see if it will be fulfilled.

The three witches in *Macbeth* prophesy that Macbeth will be king. Do they really know the future? Or does the murder only take place because they put the idea into Macbeth's head?

Tragic endings

Tragedies give a very bleak view of the world. At the end of a tragedy, the hero, and usually several other characters, are dead, and the survivors are left to start again without them. Although most tragic heroes are partly to blame for their own fates, death can be a very high price to pay for what may have seemed initially like a small failing. But in most tragedies, there is also a feeling that some good may have come out of the terrible suffering. For example, at the end of *Romeo and Juliet*, when the Prince tells the two lovers' families that their fighting has partly caused the tragedy, they finally resolve to end their feud.

When sorrows come they come not single spies But in battalions   Hamlet, IV.v.76-7

The great tragedies

Hamlet, *Othello*, *King Lear* and *Macbeth* are known as the great tragedies, and were written at the height of Shakespeare's career. The weaknesses of human beings, their potential for evil, prejudice, cruelty and greed, and the horror of madness are all explored through unforgettable characters such as the wicked Iago, the tyrannical but vulnerable Lear, the neurotic, manic-depressive Hamlet, and the cold, hard-hearted Lady Macbeth.

The supernatural

Several of the tragedies contain supernatural characters, such as ghosts and witches. For example when Macbeth has Banquo killed, Banquo's ghost appears at Macbeth's feast that evening, reminding Macbeth of his guilt.

In *Hamlet*, the ghost of Hamlet's father appears to Hamlet, urging him to avenge his murder.

Othello

Othello has a relatively straightforward plot. Othello, a general, is led to suspect that his wife, Desdemona, is having an affair with his best friend. He becomes more and more convinced, and more and more furious, until he kills her. This suspicion is created by one of Shakespeare's most evil characters, Iago, who is angry that Othello has not promoted him. He deliberately arouses Othello's doubts and uses a series of ingenious tricks to make Desdemona look guilty. Although Othello is a murderer, he is also a victim of Iago's wickedness. *Othello* is the only Shakespeare play to have a black hero. Othello is a Moor, which in Shakespeare's day meant someone from Africa.

Othello is torn between his passionate love for Desdemona and his overpowering suspicions and painful jealousy. Here, Paul Robeson plays Othello, with Mary Ure as Desdemona.

Hamlet

The plot of *Hamlet* concerns the inability of Hamlet, Prince of Denmark, to take revenge on his uncle, Claudius, who has murdered the rightful King (Hamlet's father), married the Queen, and taken the throne. Hamlet puts off killing Claudius (even though his father's ghost urges him to do so) and pretends to be mad. Hamlet accidentally kills Polonius, a lord, whose daughter Ophelia (Hamlet's ex-girlfriend) goes insane. Meanwhile, Claudius plots to kill Hamlet. At the end of the play, the Queen is killed accidentally by poison, intended for Hamlet. Hamlet is fatally wounded in a duel but finally kills Claudius before he dies.

Critics have often argued over why Hamlet delays in killing Claudius. Does he recognize that one murder cannot justify another? Or is he really mad, as he pretends to be? The wide range of possibilities means that *Hamlet* can be acted and directed in many different ways.

Go to www.usborne-quicklinks.com for a link to a Web site you may find helpful if you are studying *Hamlet*.

King Lear

King Lear is a tragedy about an unwise king. When King Lear decides to divide up his kingdom between his three daughters according to how much they love him, the youngest, Cordelia, refuses to take part, and he banishes her in fury. In fact, she is his most loving and loyal daughter. The other two, Goneril and Regan, soon reject their father and fight with each other over their lover, Edmund. But Lear does not realize his mistake until it is too late.

In *King Lear*, Shakespeare explores the difference between real and false love. Goneril and Regan both make grand speeches about their love for their father so as to win land. But only Cordelia loves her father enough to stand by him when he is in trouble, while Goneril and Regan turn against him. At first Lear is not wise enough to see this, and his family and kingdom are destroyed as a result.

King Lear with Gloucester, a loyal lord who has been blinded by Regan's husband, the Duke of Cornwall.

Macbeth

Macbeth is Shakespeare's shortest tragedy. It is a fast-moving and exciting story of a Scottish thane, or lord, who kills the King, Duncan, in order to become king himself. He also kills his friend, Banquo, in his quest for power. But guilt prevents Macbeth from enjoying the rewards of his actions, and he becomes a miserable tyrant, murdering helpless victims and condemning himself to defeat and death in battle.

At the same time, Macbeth is not an unsympathetic character. Even though he behaves evilly, he is a tortured soul, pressurized from all sides, especially by his wife, Lady Macbeth. She spurs him on to murder the King, goading him with accusations that he is not manly enough. He gradually changes from a good soldier into a terrible oppressor, but even at the end we may still feel a little sorry for him.

Strange states of mind

Characters have mental problems in several of the tragedies. They go insane with grief or with the pressure of having to make a decision. Feelings of guilt may come out in strange ways. For example, Lady Macbeth pretends to be tough and mocks Macbeth for feeling guilty about murdering the King, but her own horror is revealed when she starts sleepwalking and imagines she can see blood on her hands.

Ophelia in *Hamlet* goes insane with grief when Hamlet rejects her and kills her father, Polonius.

Will all great Neptune's ocean wash this blood Clean from my hand? Macbeth, II.ii.58-9

The Roman tragedies

Julius Caesar, *Antony and Cleopatra* and *Coriolanus*, the Roman tragedies, deal with political power. Their heroes are state leaders who have a responsibility to the people. Often, tragedy results when they fail to meet their responsibilities. However, these plays are not just about politics. They are full of personal emotions, dramatic power struggles, and brilliant writing, including some of the most famous speeches in Shakespeare's plays.

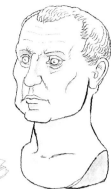

The heroes of the Roman plays were real people. Julius Caesar (above) lived from about 100 to 44BC.

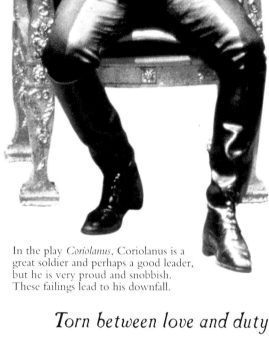

In the play *Coriolanus*, Coriolanus is a great soldier and perhaps a good leader, but he is very proud and snobbish. These failings lead to his downfall.

Politics and power

The Roman tragedies are set mainly in ancient Rome. Shakespeare based the plots on stories of real Roman heroes, but he often adapted them to make them more exciting.

The plays show how hard it is to be a political leader. Their heroes have power, but also weaknesses which make them vulnerable to being attacked or overthrown. For example, in *Antony and Cleopatra*, Antony, one of three rulers of Rome, is in love with the Egyptian Queen Cleopatra, and spends so much time in Egypt that he neglects his duties. Eventually, the Romans turn against him and he loses everything. In *Julius Caesar*, Brutus joins a conspiracy to murder Caesar (the Emperor) and to seize power, only to find that he cannot cope with the responsibilities of power himself. In each case, Shakespeare shows how easily the balance of power can be upset, and how there is always someone waiting to attack or betray a leader and seize his position.

Torn between love and duty

In Shakespeare's Roman tragedies, people often have to make difficult choices between their emotions and their responsibilities. For example, in *Antony and Cleopatra*, Antony is so in love with Cleopatra that he spends his time with her, even though he has important duties in Rome. This leads to his tragic death. Enobarbus, Antony's friend and fellow soldier, also has to make a choice. He tells Antony that duty is more important than love, but he loves Antony and wants to support him. He eventually leaves Antony in disgust, but ends up alone, dying of grief.

Antony and his friend Enobarbus in *Antony and Cleopatra*.

Comic scenes

A comic scene in the middle of a tragedy may not sound like a good idea, but most of Shakespeare's tragedies have them. They give the audience a break from harrowing scenes, and can help to make characters seem more human.

Comic scenes often involve servants or working-class people, giving a broader view of the grand setting of most tragedies. For example, in *Antony and Cleopatra*, Cleopatra's servants joke about the predictions a fortune-teller makes for them. This contrasts with the play's tragic ending, but it also reveals the relaxed atmosphere of Cleopatra's court.

Left: a comic scene from *Macbeth*. After the murder of the King, the drunken porter's joking contrasts chillingly with the atmosphere of horror.

The power of rhetoric

In Shakespeare's political plays, rhetoric (persuasive language) is very important. The characters use it to attack those in power, or to win the support of the mob (the common people of the city), which can be the key to achieving and holding onto power. A good speech is shown to be as influential as a great battle.

In *Julius Caesar*, after Caesar is murdered, the mob is at first persuaded by Brutus and the other conspirators that he deserved to die. But then Mark Antony, Caesar's friend, makes a funeral speech over Caesar's body. At first he seems to be on Brutus's side, but gradually he turns the crowd against Brutus. His speech shows that skill with words is just as valuable in politics as ambition, cunning, or military strength. The pictures below show how Antony's speech works.

Antony making his speech to the mob in a television version of *Julius Caesar*.

At first, Antony addresses the mob very politely. He knows that treating the people with respect and making them feel flattered will help him gain their attention.

Antony speaks of how noble and heroic his friend Caesar was. But, he says, if Brutus disagrees, Brutus must be right, because "Brutus is an honourable man". At this point, it seems to the crowd that Antony really believes what he is saying, and thinks that he must have been mistaken to trust Caesar.

Antony cunningly repeats the same line, "Brutus is an honourable man", so that he seems to be agreeing with Brutus. But at the same time, he keeps praising Caesar, until his praise of Brutus starts to sound sarcastic. Soon the mob begins to realize that Antony is actually criticizing Brutus, not praising him.

Although Antony is manipulating the mob, he pretends to be an innocent bystander with a humble opinion. At last, knowing what effect it will have, he tells the crowd that Caesar has left each citizen some money in his will. This starts a riot, with the mob now fully on his side and determined to attack Brutus and the conspirators.

The comedies

Shakespearean comedies aren't necessarily funny, but they do usually have happy endings. They can be divided into three main groups: "happy" comedies, which are often funny; problem plays (see page 24), which deal with more serious issues; and the romances (see page 26), which are similar to fairy tales. These two pages explore the happy comedies, from the slapstick of *The Comedy of Errors* to the sophistication of *Much Ado About Nothing* and *Twelfth Night*.

The Comedy of Errors is about two pairs of identical twins. People keep getting them mixed up.

Approximate dates when the comedies were written:

Happy comedies
The Comedy of Errors 1593–4
The Taming of the Shrew 1593–4
The Two Gentlemen of Verona 1594–5
Love's Labour's Lost 1594–5
A Midsummer Night's Dream 1595–6
The Merchant of Venice 1596–7
The Merry Wives of Windsor 1598–9
Much Ado About Nothing 1598–9
As You Like It 1599–1600
Twelfth Night 1600–01

Problem plays
Troilus and Cressida 1601–02
All's Well That Ends Well 1602–03
Measure for Measure 1603–04

Romances
Pericles 1607–08
Cymbeline 1609–10
The Winter's Tale 1610–11
The Tempest 1611–12
The Two Noble Kinsmen 1613–4

The early comedies

Shakespeare's earliest comedies use lots of jokes and slapstick to get laughs. The plot is very important, and characters are not always very realistic. In *The Comedy of Errors*, for example, the play revolves around the confusion caused when a pair of identical twins, both called Antipholus, and their twin servants, both called Dromio, are separated. The mix-ups get more and more complicated, with only the audience knowing which twin is which. In *A Midsummer Night's Dream*, fairies use a love potion to try to end two young couples' quarrels, but everyone ends up in love with the wrong person. But, as in all the happy comedies, the problems are solved and everyone gets married.

Another kind of comic device involves laughing at someone's incompetence. In *A Midsummer Night's Dream*, some workmen put on a play for the Duke's wedding. Their disastrous rehearsals and botched final performance provide lots of jokes at the actors' expense.

Fools and jesters

Some of the comedies have a fool, jester or joker, such as Puck in *A Midsummer Night's Dream* and Feste in *Twelfth Night*. They provide comic moments with jokes, songs and innuendoes. They may also act as messengers for the other characters, and offer them advice and friendship. They often make clever remarks and observations about what is happening in the play.

In *A Midsummer Night's Dream*, a magic love potion makes Titania, queen of the fairies, fall in love with Bottom, a workman, who has been given an ass's head.

The later comedies: wit and wisdom

In the later happy comedies, character becomes more important.
The main character is often a woman who uses her intelligence
and cunning to sort out a difficult situation. For example, Portia in
The Merchant of Venice has two roles. She is the romantic heroine,
waiting at home for a suitor, as required by her father's will.
But she also dresses up as a man and goes to the Duke's court
pretending to be a lawyer. There she tricks the Duke and even
her own husband, and uses her reasoning to save Antonio from
Shylock, who intends to cut off a pound of his flesh. Rosalind in
As You Like It is another witty, clever heroine.

Relationships are explored more
deeply than in the earlier comedies.
In *Much Ado About Nothing*, there are
two couples. Claudio and Hero are
young, beautiful and in love, but
when Claudio thinks Hero has been
unfaithful, he turns on her and
denounces her. They are more
conventional than the other couple,
Beatrice and Benedick, who spend
most of the play bickering and making
fun of each other, because they are
too proud to admit that they are in
love. They are the stars of the play.
Shakespeare makes the story of
conventional "true love" into the
secondary plot, and concentrates on the
more interesting, sophisticated lovers
whose relationship is more complicated.

Peggy Ashcroft and John Gielgud
play Beatrice and Benedick in a 1950
production of *Much Ado About Nothing*.

At first, Beatrice and Benedick in *Much Ado
About Nothing* argue and tease each other. Later
they are tricked into revealing their feelings.

Melancholy moments

Although the happy comedies
have happy endings, they are all
touched by elements of sadness
or tragedy. Evil characters,
such as Don John in *Much
Ado About Nothing*, who
almost destroys Claudio
and Hero, are not always
forgiven. Songs sung by
fools often contain
melancholy elements, as
when Feste in *Twelfth
Night* sings "What's to
come is still unsure...
Youth's a stuff will not
endure" and "The rain it
raineth every day".

Left: Jaques, a lord in the happy
comedy *As You Like It*, is
described as "a melancholy fellow"
because of the gloomy, cynical
view he has of life.

Love and marriage

This picture shows the dance at the end of *Much Ado About Nothing*,
when everything has been sorted out and the two couples are finally
about to get married.

Overcoming the obstacles to love is the theme of
many of the comedies. Couples flirt and fall out, and
there are lots of rude jokes and innuendoes; but order
and propriety are always restored, and everything is
rounded off with engagements or weddings, often
ending with a party or dance to celebrate. This
contrasts with the tragedies, in which relationships
that have already been formed start to fail. The happy
comedies are characterized by their hope, anticipation,
and promise of a "happy-ever-after" future.

The problem plays

The comedies *All's Well That Ends Well, Measure for Measure* and *Troilus and Cressida* are often known as the problem plays. This is partly because they deal with social and moral problems, but they are also "problematic" because they can be difficult for audiences to make sense of. Characters are hard to categorize, and plots are torn between reality and fantasy. Their dark view of life makes these plays seem particularly modern.

Is all well that ends well?

At the end of *All's Well that Ends Well*, Bertram is forced to go through with his marriage to Helena. As this production shows, Bertram does not necessarily consider this a happy ending.

Both *Measure for Measure* and *All's Well That Ends Well* end with the main characters coming together in marriage, just as in most other Shakespearean comedies. But in these plays, we may feel that perhaps marriage isn't such a happy ending.

In *All's Well*, the heroine, Helena, loves Bertram, but he thinks he's too good for her. She wins Bertram when she magically cures the dying King, and he offers her any husband she wants. But Bertram is an unwilling husband. He leaves for Italy, offering Helena an "impossible" challenge – she must get the ring off his finger and bear his child before he'll have anything to do with her.

The magical cure, and the impossible task, which Helena manages to achieve with a series of clever tricks, are fairy-tale plot devices. We might expect a fairy-tale ending too, with Bertram realizing he has loved Helena all along. But instead, he is unwillingly forced into keeping his marriage vows. The play cynically attacks the fairy-tale image of marriage. By the end, its cheerful title seems ironic.

Similarly in *Measure for Measure* (see opposite) the disgraced Angelo is forced to marry his spurned fiancée. This marriage also looks set to be far from "happy ever after".

Cynical Shakespeare

Troilus and Cressida is one of Shakespeare's most cynical plays. It tells the story of a Trojan prince, Troilus, and his love for Cressida, who betrays him for a Greek soldier, Diomedes. Like *All's Well That Ends Well* (see left), the play seems to disappoint our expectations. Troilus fails to get his revenge, and his side fails to win the war. The play ends with the assassination of Troilus's brother Hector, the leader of the Trojan army. Instead of depicting heroic deeds, the play shows greed, envy and corruption, and the futility of conflict. This grim portrayal of human nature is typical of the problem plays.

Experts think these plays were written around 1601-1604. Some critics think Shakespeare's cynicism at this time was the result of unhappiness in his own life. But it is just as likely that he was experimenting with comedy, and trying out new approaches.

This woodcut shows Troilus and Cressida, the lovers whose relationship is destroyed by betrayal.

Go to **www.usborne-quicklinks.com** for a link to a Web site with an interactive version of *Measure for Measure*, with video clips, study notes and definitions of difficult words and phrases.

Measure for Measure

Measure for Measure is the most popular and frequently performed of the problem plays.

The play is set in Vienna, where the Duke has let the city's laws slip, allowing illicit sex to flourish. He hands control to his deputy, Angelo, who he hopes will clean up Vienna for him.

Angelo condemns a young man, Claudio, to death for getting his fiancée pregnant, even though Escalus, an old and experienced judge, thinks Claudio should be freed. Claudio's sister, Isabella, a devout young woman who is about to enter a nunnery, is persuaded to plead with Angelo for mercy for her brother.

We have strict statutes and most biting laws... Which for this fourteen years we have let slip.

See that Claudio Be execute by nine tomorrow morning.

Angelo says he will spare Claudio if Isabella will sleep with him. She visits Claudio in jail and explains, but says she cannot sleep with Angelo. Then the Duke, disguised as a friar, intervenes. He persuades Mariana, Angelo's abandoned fiancée, to sleep with Angelo in the dark, so he thinks she's Isabella. Angelo orders Claudio's death anyway, but the jailers save Claudio, and show Angelo the head of a prisoner who has died.

Isabella goes to complain to the Duke about Angelo. The "friar" throws off his disguise and reveals himself as the Duke. Claudio is pardoned. Angelo is forced to marry Mariana and then condemned to death. But Mariana and Isabella plead for mercy, and Angelo is pardoned.

Be ready, Claudio, for your death tomorrow.

The devout Isabella pleads with the corrupt Angelo for her brother's life in *Measure for Measure*.

Justice and mercy

Measure for Measure looks at how laws should be applied. The Duke has been too lax in enforcing the law, but Angelo's over-strict judgement of Claudio is also inappropriate: Claudio had intended to marry his fiancée, and is a danger to no one. To make matters worse, Angelo is hypocritical. He is happy to commit the same crime as Claudio, because he thinks he can get away with it. He places more importance on his own power than on trying to make sure good prevails over bad. As he tells Isabella, "my false o'erweighs your true" (II.iv.170).

Isabella represents a more principled view of right and wrong, based on her Christian beliefs. She cannot agree to sleep with Angelo, as this is against her principles. But she pleads with him for mercy, reminding him that he would not expect God to judge him so harshly. Later, she also pleads for mercy for Angelo himself. Escalus, although he is a judge and represents the state, also thinks it is wrong to condemn Claudio. His humanity tempers his judgement.

The play does not have a clear moral, but shows that mercy is important. The title "Measure for Measure" reflects the idea that what you do to others may rebound on you. At the end, Angelo is punished exactly as he punished Claudio for the same sin, and then forgiven as Claudio has been. The play suggests that it is wise to be moderate and forgiving.

The romances

Shakespeare's late comedies, *Pericles*, *Cymbeline*, *The Winter's Tale* and *The Tempest*, are usually called the romances. They were written at the end of his career, and are different in style from his earlier comedies. Instead of focusing mainly on love and marriage, they deal with the separation and reunion of families. Their endings are characterized by homecomings, recognitions, reconciliations, and forgiveness.

Derek Jacobi as Prospero, the wizard in *The Tempest*, who controls a strange island with his magical "art". He carries a magic staff, and when he finally renounces his magic, he swears "I'll break my staff".

Influences and inspirations

The roots of Shakespeare's romances lie partly in Greek myths: stories of long journeys, monsters, magic, shipwrecks and storms. Although they deal with serious human problems, the romances are set in mythical worlds, where supernatural events, magic and unlikely coincidences are commonplace.

The masque performed in *The Tempest*.

The romances were also influenced by masques. These entertainments, consisting of song, dance, mime and dialogue, were performed at court for the monarch. Shakespeare used masques or masque-like sequences in all the romances. This may have been because late in his career, his theatre company often used an indoor theatre, where it was easier to arrange special effects.

Shakespeare and Prospero's "art"

In *The Tempest*, Prospero, the exiled Duke of Milan, is stranded on an island, where he uses magic, or "art" to control events. The opening storm has been called up by what he calls "my so potent art". Critics have suggested that Prospero represents Shakespeare and the "art" represents the art of the writer, who conjures up imaginary worlds and controls the characters in them. *The Tempest* was probably the last play Shakespeare wrote without a collaborator. At the end of the play, Prospero promises to give up his art and says "I'll drown my book". Some critics think this is Shakespeare's own farewell to his writing career.

Go to **www.usborne-quicklinks.com** for a link to a Web site where you can read a director's insights into the characters and themes of *A Winter's Tale*.

Fairy tale and fantasy

The themes, settings and characters in Shakespeare's romances often seem like those of traditional fairy tales. For example, in *Cymbeline*, the heroine, Imogen, has a wicked stepmother, a familiar folk-tale figure, who tries to kill her. *The Tempest* has two supernatural creatures, a flying spirit called Ariel and a subhuman monster called Caliban. As well as resembling a fairy-tale monster, Caliban may represent Elizabethan ideas about the inhabitants of newly-discovered lands. Some of the plays openly refer to their fairy-tale patterns. For example, in *The Winter's Tale*, the young Prince Mamillius says "A sad tale's best for winter". In *Pericles* a "presenter" or narrator, the poet John Gower, says he will "sing a song that old was sung", and goes on to describe the action of the play as if he were telling us a story.

Right: Caliban, the half-human monster, in a film version of *The Tempest*. Prospero calls him a "poisonous slave".

Sea stories

In the romances, characters often go on sea voyages. For example, in *Pericles*, Pericles leaves his kingdom and travels from island to island because of a death sentence against him. On his travels he finds a wife, Thaisa. Their daughter, Marina, is born at sea, but all three soon become separated from each other.

In *The Tempest*, Prospero lands on an island after being cast out to sea by his enemies. Twelve years later, he uses magic to create a huge storm, causing his enemies to be shipwrecked on the island. In *The Winter's Tale*, Leontes's baby daughter is sent away and washed up on a foreign shore, where she grows up. Storms at sea often cause characters to become separated, or to meet each other again. This helps to give the romances a strong sense of human helplessness in the face of the greater powers of magic, nature or the gods.

Reconciliation and rebirth

Although the romances contain potentially tragic events, such as shipwrecks, disappearances and separations, a tragic outcome is prevented. Instead, conflicts are healed and sins are forgiven. Families and friends are united, exiles return home and characters who were believed to be dead are found alive. The atmosphere of forgiveness is summed up in the phrase from *Cymbeline*, "Pardon's the word to all" (V.vi.424).

These happy, yet often solemn endings have a strong symbolic meaning. The reunited lovers represent the regeneration of society, guaranteeing a brighter future. The resurrections are symbols of rebirth and renewal, and the forgiveness of the final scenes is symbolic of the healing power of love and mercy.

A picture of a ship in a storm from a 1709 edition of *The Tempest*. Sea journeys and storms play an important part in most of the romances, particularly *The Winter's Tale* and *Pericles*.

We are such stuff As dreams are made on...   *The Tempest*, IV.i.156-7

The earlier history plays

This list is a guide to the approximate dates when the history plays were written:

Henry VI, Part I 1589-90
Henry VI, Parts 2 and *3* 1590-1
Richard III 1592-3
Richard II 1595-6
King John 1596-7
Henry IV, Parts I and *2* 1597-8
Henry V 1598-9
Henry VIII 1612-3

The history plays are more than just historical events acted out on stage. They are dramatic works which use history as a starting point. Instead of concentrating on facts, they examine the individuals who make history, look at how power is lost and won, and ask the question, "What makes a good king?"

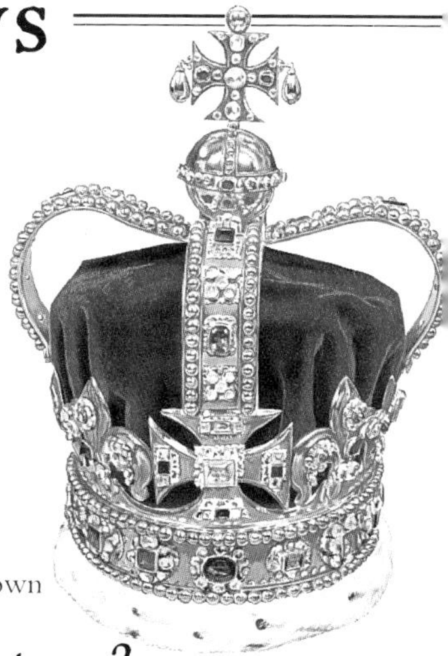

A 14th-century English crown

Is the king sacred?

The concept of the Chain of Being (see page 6) suggested that everyone had a strict place in society, which was established by God. The monarch was seen as God's chosen representative, so to oppose, or even worse overthrow, a king might also be seen as a rebellion against God.

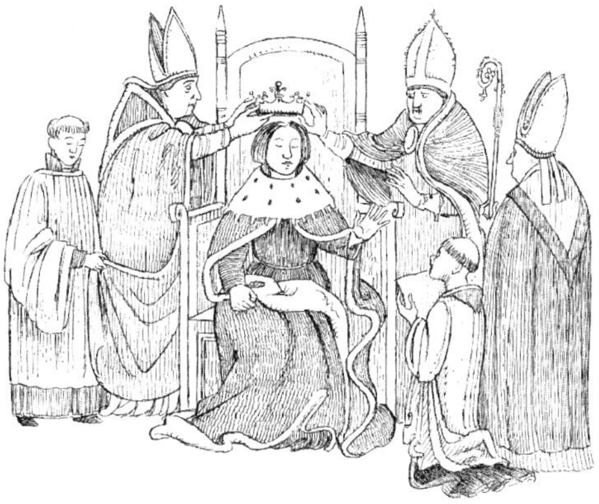

This picture, based on a mediaeval painting, shows Edward II being crowned in a religious ceremony.

Shakespeare was certainly aware of the idea that kingship was sacred. The history plays contain many speeches about it. In *Richard II*, for example, the king refers to his "right" to rule: "Not all the water in the rough rude sea/ Can wash the balm from an anointed king./ The breath of worldly men cannot depose/ The deputy elected by the Lord." (III.ii.50-3). But Richard is a weak king and *is* eventually overthrown. Shakespeare shows that, despite his sacredness, a bad king can be, and often is, replaced. Although he may claim he has a right to rule, a king must also protect his position of power.

What period of history?

Shakespeare's history plays reflect real periods in history, but he didn't write them in chronological order. The first group of plays he wrote, *Henry VI, Parts 1, 2* and *3* and *Richard III*, covers the period from 1422 to 1485, when the Wars of the Roses raged in England between the families, or "houses", of Lancaster and York.

The second main group of plays, *Richard II, Henry IV, Parts 1* and *2* and *Henry V* (see page 30), looks at an earlier period in history, from 1377 to 1422, and covers the events leading up to the Wars of the Roses.

There are two other history plays that do not fit into these groups (see page 31). *King John* is about John's reign in 1199-1216, and *Henry VIII* covers part of Henry's reign, which began in 1509.

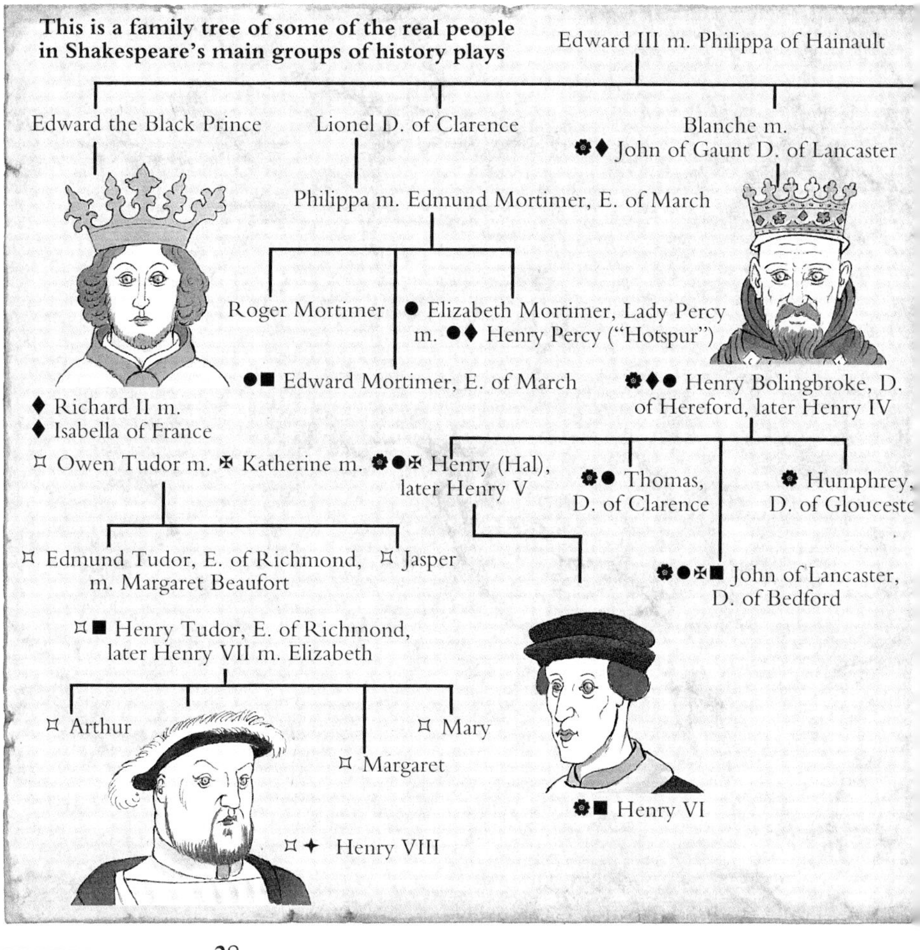
This is a family tree of some of the real people in Shakespeare's main groups of history plays
Edward III m. Philippa of Hainault
Edward the Black Prince
Lionel D. of Clarence
Blanche m.
✿♦ John of Gaunt D. of Lancaster
Philippa m. Edmund Mortimer, E. of March
Roger Mortimer
● Elizabeth Mortimer, Lady Percy m. ●♦ Henry Percy ("Hotspur")
●■ Edward Mortimer, E. of March
✿♦● Henry Bolingbroke, D. of Hereford, later Henry IV
♦ Richard II m.
♦ Isabella of France
¤ Owen Tudor m. ✠ Katherine m. ✿●✠ Henry (Hal), later Henry V
✿● Thomas, D. of Clarence
✿ Humphrey, D. of Glouceste
¤ Edmund Tudor, E. of Richmond, m. Margaret Beaufort
¤ Jasper
✿●✠■ John of Lancaster, D. of Bedford
¤■ Henry Tudor, E. of Richmond, later Henry VII m. Elizabeth
¤ Arthur
¤ Mary
¤ Margaret
✿■ Henry VI
¤✦ Henry VIII

Sources

When Henry VII became king in 1485, he had some historical books, or "chronicles", written to emphasize the unrest of England during the Wars of the Roses, and the peace that the Tudor monarchs had brought. Shakespeare used the chronicle by Edward Hall as the main source for his early history plays.

Because this chronicle was written as propaganda to please the Tudor monarchs, it told a biased version of events. For example, Shakespeare's *Richard III* shows an evil, murderous king, but today some historians have argued that the real Richard may not have been a murderer at all.

The Wars of the Roses got their name from the emblems of the two opposing sides: the red rose of Lancaster and the white rose of York.

Henry VI, Parts 1, 2 and 3

The Henry VI plays look at the problems of kingship, and at what happens when a king does not have the strength to rule effectively. Henry VI is a kind, gentle and religious man, but a useless leader. He cannot exert authority over the rebels who threaten him. This leads to disorder, civil war and Henry's own death.

Rebellion against Henry is shown to disrupt the state and lead to chaos. But on the other hand Henry is portrayed as a weak king who is himself partly responsible for the chaos. Shakespeare does not warn that kings should not be overthrown, Instead, he simply shows how a weak king lays himself open to attack.

Richard III

Shakespeare presented Richard III as a hunchback because, in Elizabethan times, disabilities were often seen as a sign of the devil. His physical deformity would have added to the impression of evil.

Richard III is a powerful portrait of an ambitious and evil man, and Richard is Shakespeare's first really memorable character. He engages the audience with his soliloquies and asides, often making humorous comments about the atrocities he has just committed. The play charts Richard's murderous path as he makes his way to the top. After he becomes king at the end of Act III, however, Richard becomes less sure of himself. He grows isolated and lonely, and finds it harder to enjoy his own evil.

The symbols below are used in the tree to show which plays historical figures appear in, and which house they belonged to. For example, Edward, Duke of Aumerle, appears in *Richard II* and *Henry V*, and belonged to the House of York.

⊛♦ Edmund of Langley, D. of York
m. ♦ Duchess of York

Thomas of Woodstock

⊛♦✠ Edward, D. of Aumerle, D. of York

⊛✠ Richard, E. of Cambridge m. Anne Mortimer

⊛■ Richard Plantagenet, D. of York m. O Cecily, D. of York

⊛O Edward IV

⊛ Elizabeth

⊛■ Edmund, E. of Rutland

⊛■O George, D. of Clarence

⊛■O Richard, D. of Gloucester, later Richard III

Key to plays
♦ *Richard II*
● *Henry IV, 1 and 2*
✠ *Henry V*
■ *Henry VI, 1, 2 and 3*
O *Richard III*
✦ *Henry VIII*

Key to houses
✿ House of Lancaster
⊛ House of York
¤ House of Tudor

Key to abbreviations
D. Duke/Duchess
E. Earl
m. married

...let us sit upon the ground, And tell sad stories of the death of kings

Richard II, III.ii.151-2

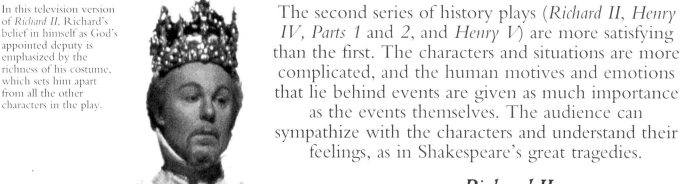

In this television version of *Richard II*, Richard's belief in himself as God's appointed deputy is emphasized by the richness of his costume, which sets him apart from all the other characters in the play.

The second series of history plays (*Richard II*, *Henry IV, Parts 1* and *2*, and *Henry V*) are more satisfying than the first. The characters and situations are more complicated, and the human motives and emotions that lie behind events are given as much importance as the events themselves. The audience can sympathize with the characters and understand their feelings, as in Shakespeare's great tragedies.

Richard II

In *Richard II*, Richard II loses his crown to Henry Bolingbroke in a military coup, although the play has no battle scenes. It is a study of the two men, and the different worlds they represent.

In this picture Richard II holds an orb, a ball with a cross on top, symbol of the sacredness of the king.

Richard II is a weak king. He is extravagant and arrogant, and sees himself as God's representative, with a sacred right to rule (see page 28). His actions (confiscating land and money, and banishing people he dislikes) upset the noblemen whose support he really needs.

Eventually the nobles give their support to the rebel Henry Bolingbroke, who plans to seize the throne. Bolingbroke is not a very likeable character, but he has the qualities which a good king needs. He is far more practical, ambitious and calculating than Richard.

However, as Richard loses his grip on the crown and comes to accept his downfall, the audience is made to feel greater sympathy for him. He shows himself to be a deeply spiritual and moral man, who is simply unsuited to being a monarch. Bolingbroke's coldness makes him seem less likeable than Richard, but the audience can see that he will make a better king. In this play, Shakespeare explores how different people cope with power, and what personal qualities they need to do so.

Uneasy lies the head that wears a crown

Henry IV, Part 2, III.i.31

Go to **www.usborne-quicklinks.com** for a link to a Web site where you can find studies of *Henry IV, Part 1* and *Henry V*.

Henry IV: Hal, the prodigal son

In *Henry IV, Parts 1* and *2*, Bolingbroke is now the king, but the plays concentrate on his son, Prince Hal. Hal has a choice of two ways of life: the irresponsible lifestyle of his drunken, debauched friend Falstaff, spent in a tavern at Eastcheap in London, or the virtue, responsibility and good example expected of a prince.

At first, Hal spends his time with Falstaff. At Eastcheap, he is free to make mistakes and to learn about the kind of people he will eventually rule. But at the end of *Part 1*, Hal kills his cousin Hotspur, who has rebelled against the King. In a speech over Hotspur's body, he admires his rival's bold, warlike qualities. At the end of *Part 2*, Hal is crowned Henry V, and brutally rejects Falstaff: "I know thee not, old man" (V.v.47). He takes on the responsibilities of leadership, but only through growing more hard-hearted.

The scene on the left is from *Henry IV, Part I*. It shows Falstaff, who has already proved himself to be a coward in battle, making a mockery of military codes of conduct by pretending to have killed the already dead Hotspur.

Henry V: Hal as hero

In *Henry V*, Hal is presented as an effective king. He keeps the peace at home, is devout, and fights for land abroad, leading his men with a stirring battle-cry: "Follow your spirit, and upon this charge/ Cry, 'God for Harry! England and Saint George!'" (III.i.33-34). Yet his character is not always sympathetic. Since his rejection of Falstaff, Hal seems to have grown colder and lost his more human side. The play questions whether a king can combine being a good man with being a good ruler.

All England

In most of the later history plays, political intrigues and glorious battles are contrasted with scenes from ordinary life. The Boar's Head Tavern at Eastcheap which is visited by Falstaff and Hal, and rural Gloucestershire are typical examples. An array of characters, from petty criminals to bumbling magistrates, represent the diversity of English society.

Falstaff drinking in the Boar's Head Tavern.

These scenes offer opportunities for comedy, but they also show how the main events of the plays are not only personal tragedies (or triumphs) for the main characters, but are also national events which affect ordinary people. For example, in *Henry IV, Part 2*, Falstaff recruits men for battle. Falstaff accepts bribes and excuses making the scene comic, but his jokes remind us that innocent men will die.

Odd ones out

Henry VIII and *King John* are one-off history plays which do not belong to a historical series.

Henry VIII shows various episodes in the King's life. It can seem more like a romance (see page 26) than a history play.

King John covers John's reign (1199-1216). It explores some of the same themes as the other history plays, especially the question of the king's right to rule. John causes the death of his nephew Arthur, who also has a claim to the throne, and is then murdered himself.

King John, taken from a medieval manuscript.

Shakespeare's poems and songs

When Shakespeare was alive, poetry was considered the most artistic form of writing. Shakespeare's most famous poems are his sonnets, a sequence of short poems about love, fame and a mysterious relationship. Poets usually depended on patrons, aristocratic friends who supported and promoted them. Shakespeare's poems are dedicated to the rich man who was his patron.

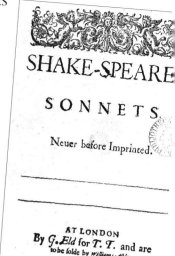

The title page of the first edition of Shakespeare's sonnets. They are dedicated to a mysterious "Mr. W. H.", who may have been Shakespeare's patron, Henry Wriothesley (see opposite page).

The sonnets are famous for their beautiful images and descriptions of nature. This illustration of a plant is based on one from an Elizabethan herbal (a book of medicinal plants).

The sonnets

Shakespeare's collection, or sequence, of 154 sonnets was first published in 1609. Around this time, sonnet sequences were very fashionable. They often told a love story, with individual names disguised. For example, the poet Philip Sidney (1554-1586) wrote a sonnet sequence called *Astrophel and Stella*, in which "Stella" may refer to a real woman, Lady Penelope Rich.

Shakespeare's sonnet sequence seems to be about his love for two people - a young man (possibly a patron) and an older woman. Experts still argue about whether these were real people, and whether the sonnets tell us anything about Shakespeare's life, or whether he made the story up. The first 126 sonnets record the poet's love for his friend, sometimes complaining that he is not loved in return, or even that the friend prefers another poet. The later sonnets, 127 to 154, address a lady, known as the "dark lady". She has betrayed the poet by loving other men, including the poet's young friend.

What is a sonnet?

A sonnet is a short poem with fourteen lines and a strict rhyme scheme. It was introduced to England from Italy in the 16th century, and has been used by English poets ever since.

There are several kinds of sonnets, each with a different rhyme scheme. The kind Shakespeare wrote, shown below, is now known as the Shakespearean sonnet.

These letters show how the sonnet rhymes - line **a** rhymes with line **a**, **b** with **b** and so on. Shakespeare uses this rhyme scheme in almost all his sonnets.

This sonnet, number 18, talks about someone's beauty, which is even more perfect than a summer day.

After the first eight lines, there is often a change of direction and a new idea is introduced.

a	*Shall I compare thee to a summer's day?*
b	*Thou art more lovely and more temperate.*
a	*Rough winds do shake the darling buds of May,*
b	*And summer's lease hath all too short a date.*
c	*Sometime too hot the eye of heaven shines,*
d	*And often is his gold complexion dimmed,*
c	*And every fair from fair sometime declines,*
d	*By chance or nature's changing course untrimmed;*
e	*But thy eternal summer shall not fade*
f	*Nor lose possession of that fair thou ow'st;*
e	*Nor shall death brag thou wander'st in his shade*
f	*When in eternal lines to time thou grow'st.*
g	*So long as men can breathe, or eyes can see,*
g	*So long lives this, and this gives life to thee.*

Nature, the weather and the seasons are used as metaphors (see page 34) throughout Shakespeare's sonnets.

Shakespeare usually uses the last two lines of a sonnet to make a statement. Here he says that this poem will immortalize the beautiful person he writes about.

Unlike the rest of the lines, the last two lines are a rhyming couplet - two lines that rhyme with each other.

Go to **www.usborne-quicklinks.com** for a link to a Web site where you can choose a Shakespeare sonnet to send as an e-card.

Songs from the plays

There are songs in many of Shakespeare's plays, especially the comedies. They are often sung by clowns, fairies or country people to celebrate the seasons, or to mark special occasions, such as weddings and funerals. Shakespeare didn't always invent these songs himself. Some of them were already popular at the time, and he borrowed or adapted them for use in his plays.

Feste (right), the clown in *Twelfth Night*, sings a song (below) to entertain the other characters. The song says that life is short and we must enjoy it while we can.

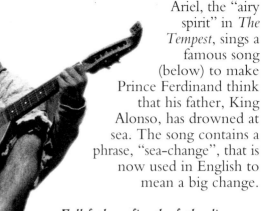

What is love? 'Tis not hereafter,
Present mirth hath present laughter,
What's to come is still unsure.
In delay there lies no plenty,
Then come kiss me, sweet and twenty,
Youth's a stuff will not endure.

Ariel, the "airy spirit" in *The Tempest*, sings a famous song (below) to make Prince Ferdinand think that his father, King Alonso, has drowned at sea. The song contains a phrase, "sea-change", that is now used in English to mean a big change.

Full fathom five thy father lies,
Of his bones are coral made;
Those are pearls that were his eyes;
Nothing of him that doth fade
But doth suffer a sea-change
Into something rich and strange...

Shakespeare and his patrons

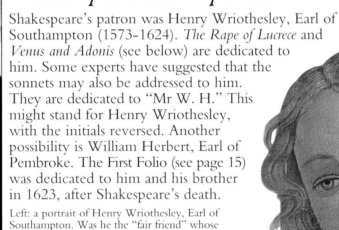

Shakespeare's patron was Henry Wriothesley, Earl of Southampton (1573-1624). *The Rape of Lucrece* and *Venus and Adonis* (see below) are dedicated to him. Some experts have suggested that the sonnets may also be addressed to him. They are dedicated to "Mr W. H." This might stand for Henry Wriothesley, with the initials reversed. Another possibility is William Herbert, Earl of Pembroke. The First Folio (see page 15) was dedicated to him and his brother in 1623, after Shakespeare's death.

Left: a portrait of Henry Wriothesley, Earl of Southampton. Was he the "fair friend" whose beauty Shakespeare praised so highly in the sonnets?

Other poems

Shakespeare wrote several poems besides the sonnets. His first major poem, *Venus and Adonis*, was published in 1593, and may have been written the previous summer when the theatres were closed due to plague. In the poem, the goddess Venus tries to woo the beautiful Adonis and distract him from his hunting. Eventually she finds him killed by a boar. A year later, Shakespeare published *The Rape of Lucrece*. These two poems were his first works to be printed. His other poetry includes songs, *The Lover's Complaint* (1609), a pastoral (country) poem about a jilted lover and *The Phoenix and the Turtle* (1601), a poem celebrating the mystery of married love.

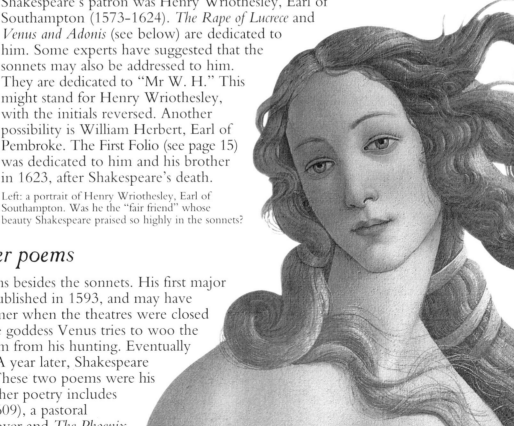

Venus, the Roman goddess of love, often appears in art and literature and would have been familiar to Shakespeare's readers. This picture of Venus is from *The Birth of Venus* by the Italian painter Botticelli (1444-1510).

Shakespeare's language

Shakespeare's use of language made him one of the greatest writers in the world. With extraordinary skill and poetic imagination, he could set vivid scenes, express powerful emotions and reveal character in highly original ways. Many of his phrases have become part of our everyday language.

Ways with words

Writers often use literary devices, or special ways of using words. These devices can help to express complex ideas, emphasize what is being said, or describe something in a memorable or exciting way. One of the main devices Shakespeare uses is imagery – using images, or "figures of speech", to describe things. For example, Hamlet uses the phrase "a sea of troubles" to describe his problems. This image makes us think of the sea, and we can imagine Hamlet's problems surging towards him like the tide, or swallowing him up like a sinking ship. Metaphors and similes (see below) are two types of imagery.

In this speech from the end of *Antony and Cleopatra*, Antony has killed himself, wrongly believing Cleopatra to be dead. Cleopatra describes him to a Roman soldier, Dolabella, who guards her. The speech contains some of the literary devices Shakespeare uses most often. Difficult words are explained at the bottom of the page.

Antony, the great Roman leader and lover of Cleopatra, the Egyptian queen.

Cleopatra uses amazing figures of speech, involving stars, planets and thunder, to describe Antony's greatness.

A **simile** (pronounced *sim*-ill-ee) is a comparison of one thing with another, usually using the words "as" or "like". Here Cleopatra says that when he was angry, Antony was as, or like, thunder, meaning that he could be impressively loud and frightening.

A **metaphor** describes something as if it were something else. Cleopatra describes Antony's bounty (generosity) as a season, autumn, that could be "reaped". This is not a factual description of Antony, but the metaphor works by making us think of overflowing richness and warmth.

His legs bestrid the ocean; his reared arm
Crested the world. His voice was propertied
As all the tuned spheres, and that to friends;
But when he meant to quail and shake the orb,
He was as rattling thunder. For his bounty,
There was no winter in't; an autumn 'twas,
That grew the more by reaping. His delights
Were dolphin-like; they showed his back above
The element they lived in. In his livery
Walked crowns and crownets. Realms and islands were
As plates dropped from his pocket.

Antony and Cleopatra, V.ii.81–91

Alliteration means repeating the same sound at the beginnings of words that are close together, to emphasize them, as in "crowns and crownets" and "delights were dolphin-like".

Hyperbole (pronounced hi-*per*-ber-lee) means exaggerating. Of course Antony was not really this enormous, but Cleopatra's exaggeration shows the size of his personality, his great political influence on the world, and the extent of her love for him.

Assonance is the repeated use of the same vowel sound in words that are close together. 'Quail' and 'shake' sound similar, and are used together to emphasize Antony's power.

bestrid stood astride
reared raised
crested topped
was propertied had properties, or qualities
tuned spheres the seven spheres, or planets, which were thought to give out heavenly music

quail to frighten
orb the world
bounty generosity
in't in it
'twas it was
delights the delightful things about him

element one of the four elements, fire, earth, air and water.
livery someone's servants or followers
crowns kings
crownets princes or other royalty
plates silver coins

Shakespeare's language can seem difficult and strange at first. Go to **www.usborne-quicklinks.com** for a link to a Web site where you'll find a helpful introduction, with a short wordlist and a guide to making notes on the plays.

Language and character

The way characters speak and the language they use tell us a great deal about them and their situation. For example, here are two characters who speak very differently.

John of Gaunt, in *Richard II*, is an old lord who disapproves of the King's extravagant ways. This is the opening of a speech which uses a sequence of beautiful metaphors, expressing strong patriotic emotions. The majestic rhythm, long words and poetic style reflect Gaunt's age and status.

This royal throne of kings, this sceptred isle,
This earth of majesty, this seat of Mars,
This other Eden, demi-paradise,
This fortress built by nature for herself
Against infection and the hand of war...

Richard II, II.i.40-44

In *Henry IV, Part 1*, the hostess of the tavern is a working-class woman. Her low social status is reflected in this speech, which is in prose, using simple words, a rough, lively rhythm, and no metaphors or similes.

I am no thing to thank God on. I would thou
shouldst know it. I am an honest man's wife; and
setting thy knighthood aside, thou art a knave to
call me so.

Henry IV, Part 1, III.iii.118-121.

Sometimes, a character is associated with a certain kind of imagery. In *Macbeth*, for example, much of the imagery that Macbeth uses is concerned with blood, and in Act III he conjures up a horrific image of himself stranded in a river of blood. This reveals his terrible guilt and shows that he cannot stop thinking about the murder he has committed.

It is the bloody business...   II.i.48-9

Will all great Neptune's ocean wash this blood
Clean from my hand?   II.ii.58-9

It will have blood, they say.
Blood will have blood.   III.iv.122

...I am in blood
Stepped in so far that,
should I wade no more,
Returning were as
tedious as go o'er.

III.iv.135-7

Macbeth, covered with blood after the murder of the King. Throughout the play, he describes himself as stained, soaked or swimming in blood, symbolizing his guilt.

Shakespeare's legacy

Many of Shakespeare's expressions, or idioms, have become part of the English language. People often use Shakespearean idioms without realizing it.

"You'll eat us out of house and home if you're not careful!"
("He hath eaten me out of house and home." *Henry IV, Part 2*, II.i.75-6)

"There's a method in my madness."
("Though this be madness, yet there is method in 't." *Hamlet*, II.ii.207-8)

"There's no need to lay it on with a trowel!"
("Well said. That was laid on with a trowel." *As You Like It*, I.ii.99)

"Well, the world's your oyster now."
("Why then, the world's mine oyster." *The Merry Wives of Windsor*, II.ii.4-5)

In Shakespeare's time, there were no dictionaries. People could spell words however they wanted, and sometimes made up new ones. Over 2,000 of the words Shakespeare used had not been recorded before, and he may have made many of them up. Here are a few of the words first used by Shakespeare which are still in use today.

leapfrog

submerged

countless

fretful

barefaced

dwindle

lonely

Issues in Shakespeare

Many of Shakespeare's works deal with issues which have as much relevance today as in Elizabethan times. For example, *The Taming of the Shrew* deals with the battle between the sexes, and *Othello* and *The Merchant of Venice* draw attention to racial issues. But did Shakespeare really have any social or moral messages for his audience, or was he simply recording human life and culture as he saw it? These pages look at some of the issues Shakespeare raised, and the way he treated them.

Rosalind in *As You Like It*, disguised as a boy called Ganymede.

Imogen, the heroine in *Cymbeline*, like many of Shakespeare's heroines, disguises herself as a boy. Imogen has many adventures, but her story ends with a return to her husband.

Was Shakespeare a feminist?

Many of Shakespeare's female characters are intelligent and strong-willed. They seem freer and more independent than most women of his time actually were. Rosalind, the heroine of *As You Like It*, disguises herself as a boy, escapes from her power-crazed uncle, survives in the forest and finds her lover again. Portia in *The Merchant of Venice* provides a brilliantly clever solution to an apparently insoluble problem. Cleopatra in *Antony and Cleopatra* is an Egyptian queen whose powerful personality threatens the leadership of Rome.

Even so, most of Shakespeare's heroines are shown in relation to men, and find happiness through husbands or lovers. For Rosalind, a happy ending means engagement to her lover, Orlando. Portia uses her intelligence to save her husband's friend before settling down to become a wife, and Cleopatra kills herself when her beloved Antony dies.

Shakespeare wrote about the kinds of women that the women in his audience liked to watch. His female characters are varied and exciting, which also helps to make the plays exciting. But he also reflected Elizabethan values in showing love and marriage to be the main focus of women's lives.

Lady Macbeth appears to be a "strong" woman. But her lust for power can only be achieved through her husband, Macbeth. Without her marriage, she would be powerless.

...there is nothing either good or bad but thinking makes it so. *Hamlet*, II.ii.251-2

Anti-semitism (prejudice against Jews) was common in Elizabethan England. Was Shakespeare prejudiced? Go to **www.usborne-quicklinks.com** for a link to a Web site that offers one view.

Ghosts and gods

Shakespeare grew up in an actively Christian England. Protestants and Catholics had different forms of Christian worship, and were at war with each other in some European countries.

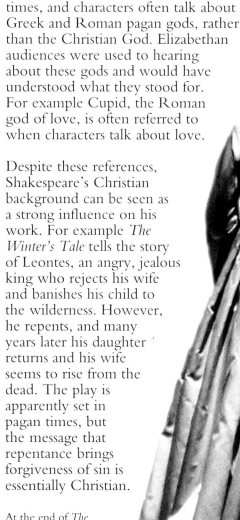

Cupid, the Roman god of love, who is often mentioned by characters in Shakespeare's plays.

Many people also believed in occult and supernatural phenomena, as they do today. Their beliefs are reflected in Shakespeare's works. Even in plays set in Christian countries, characters are just as likely to be influenced by supernatural forces, such as witches, ghosts or magical prophecies, as by Christian teaching.

Many of Shakespeare's plays are set in ancient times, and characters often talk about Greek and Roman pagan gods, rather than the Christian God. Elizabethan audiences were used to hearing about these gods and would have understood what they stood for. For example Cupid, the Roman god of love, is often referred to when characters talk about love.

Despite these references, Shakespeare's Christian background can be seen as a strong influence on his work. For example *The Winter's Tale* tells the story of Leontes, an angry, jealous king who rejects his wife and banishes his child to the wilderness. However, he repents, and many years later his daughter returns and his wife seems to rise from the dead. The play is apparently set in pagan times, but the message that repentance brings forgiveness of sin is essentially Christian.

At the end of *The Winter's Tale*, Leontes is terrified and amazed to find that a statue of his wife Hermione, whom he had thought was dead, is actually Hermione herself.

Racial prejudice

In several plays, racial prejudice is shown in action. When Othello, a Moor (African), marries the white Desdemona, her father is horrified, and Othello shows his insecurity when he suspects her of preferring a white lover. Shylock in *The Merchant of Venice* is despised for being Jewish, and he in turn is hostile to the Christians.

Shakespeare shows us that victims of prejudice feel pain and resentment. For example, Shylock questions the grounds of the prejudice against him: "Hath not a Jew hands, organs, dimensions, senses, affections, passions; fed with the same food, hurt with the same weapons, subject to the same diseases, healed by the same means, warmed and cooled by the same winter and summer as a Christian is?" (III.i,55-59). But Shakespeare is also harshly realistic. Othello ends up dead, and Shylock is forced to give up his faith and become a Christian. Instead of spelling out what is right and wrong, Shakespeare shows all the destructive power of human prejudice and leaves us to come to our own conclusions.

Shakespeare through the ages

Since Shakespeare's time, performances of his plays have varied enormously in style and technique. Each era has reflected its own preoccupations in its adaptations and treatments of his works, from early rewritings of the plays to the experimental methods of the modern age.

Restoration Shakespeare

From 1642 to 1660, England's theatres were closed by the Puritans, who disapproved of playgoing. They were reopened with the Restoration of the Monarchy in 1660, when Charles II came home from exile in France. The Restoration brought a whole new style of drama to the English stage. New theatres were built, actresses appeared on the stage for the first time and hundreds of new plays were written. Restoration drama was not as universal or timeless as Shakespeare's, but it did reflect the postwar mood of celebration and sophistication.

A portrait of the Restoration actor Thomas Betterton

When Shakespeare's plays were performed, they were heavily adapted by playwrights such as William Davenant (1606-68) and Nahum Tate (1652-1715). In Tate's version of *King Lear*, Cordelia has an affair with Edgar, and Lear and Cordelia are saved in a happy ending. Tate's *King Lear* was very popular and was performed regularly for over 150 years.

The 18th century and David Garrick

Shakespeare performances in the 18th century were dominated by David Garrick (1717-79). He was the first in a long line of "actor-managers" who ran theatres and produced and starred in performances. Shakespeare was his hero, and he set about producing as many of the plays as possible and bringing them to a wide audience. He also developed a new, more relaxed, realistic way of speaking his lines which replaced the formal acting style that had gone before. However, Garrick also often rewrote and adapted the plays. Few performances used Shakespeare's original text.

In 1769 Garrick organized a "Shakespeare Jubilee" to celebrate Shakespeare at his birthplace, Stratford-upon-Avon. This was the beginning of the Shakespeare industry that thrives in Stratford today.

David Garrick playing Benedick in *Much Ado About Nothing*. During his career, Garrick played almost all the main male roles in Shakespeare's plays.

16TH CENTURY

Most performances were in open-air theatres with no lighting and not much scenery.

17TH CENTURY

Shakespeare's plays were adapted to suit the sophisticated, fashionable tastes that developed during the Restoration.

18TH CENTURY

Garrick developed a new, natural acting style and introduced more realistic scenery.

19TH CENTURY

Historical accuracy and realistic scenery were taken to extremes in grand, extravagant productions.

20TH CENTURY

Directors attempted to recreate the Elizabethan stage, or experimented with modern settings and designs.

The 19th century

In the 19th century, Shakespeare became hugely popular. There was a trend for restoring the plays to their original texts. For example, Nahum Tate's *King Lear* (see opposite) was finally replaced by an older version in 1838. There was also an obsession with historical accuracy and period detail. Producers would attempt to recreate ancient Egypt for *Antony and Cleopatra*, or medieval Scotland for *Macbeth*. Performances were elaborate, with very realistic sets and hundreds of extras for crowd and battle scenes.

Edmund Kean was the most famous actor of the early 19th century. In the later Victorian era, Henry Irving and Herbert Beerbohm Tree produced and starred in sumptuous productions which took realism to new heights. Sets might include real waterfalls or streams, or live animals.

Edmund Kean as Othello. The poet Coleridge wrote that seeing Kean act was so exciting that it was like "reading Shakespeare by flashes of lightning".

Ellen Terry playing Lady Macbeth. Terry was the greatest actress of the late 19th century, and often played lead female roles opposite Henry Irving.

The 20th century

The end of the 19th century saw a backlash against the elaborate historical style, and a return to the Elizabethan style, with very little scenery and as much of the original text as possible. This style has been popular throughout the 20th century, but there have also been many experimental or "avant-garde" interpretations, including modern-dress productions, all-female casts, and modern props such as bicycles, cars, skateboards and telephones.

Above: a scene from a modern production of *A Midsummer Night's Dream.*

In this production, the characters wear a variety of modern costumes.

John Gielgud playing Hamlet at the New Theatre in 1934. Other famous 20th-century theatre stars include Laurence Olivier, Peggy Ashcroft and Judi Dench.

The 20th century has also been characterized by many new ways of presenting and understanding Shakespeare. His works have been translated into dozens of languages and his plays are now performed all over the world. Shakespeare has also inspired many plays, films, books and other works of art (see page 46) and his works are studied by millions of students and experts in schools and universities.

Acting and directing styles

The director of a play controls the artistic side of a production. His or her job is to decide how to interpret the play, and to make sure that all the elements work together to make a convincing and exciting performance. The style in which a director chooses to stage a play can make a huge difference to the play's meaning. Costumes, sets, props, sound and lighting, and the way each character is portrayed, can vary enormously between different productions of the same play. Sometimes even the text is changed.

The modern costumes in this production of *Romeo and Juliet* may help the audience to identify with the characters in the play.

Interpretation

Although the script for a play is usually written by a playwright, the director and actors in a production have to decide how to present it. They can emphasize some parts and cut others, decide what costumes, scenery and props to use, and change the setting. This is called interpretation. Even the simplest production is a unique interpretation, showing only how a particular director and team of actors understand the play.

For example, a production of *Measure for Measure* (see page 25) could choose to show Angelo and Isabella, the main characters, in very different ways. Is Angelo a heartless, corrupt politician cruelly imposing his will on the poor, innocent Isabella? Or is he a victim, caught between his desire to do the right thing and his helpless lust for the prim Isabella? It's up to the director to decide, and to help the actors play their parts convincingly.

Modern messages

Directors sometimes use a Shakespeare play to put across a message, or to raise a modern issue. For example, when *The Merchant of Venice* was performed in previous centuries, the Jewish Shylock was played as a villain. Anti-Semitism (hostility towards Jews) was more common then. However, a modern audience is more aware of racism and may feel sympathy for Shylock. Instead of ignoring this, a director might choose to explore it. Shylock could be played as a more sympathetic character, or could be shown as a victim of racism. Costumes and props could be used to suggest a modern setting in which racism would be unacceptable.

Two different 20th-century Shylocks: (left) Frank Benson in 1904, and (right) Dustin Hoffman in 1989.

Go to **www.usborne-quicklinks.com** for a link to a Web site where you can read about a director making choices and solving problems in a college production of *Romeo and Juliet*.

Two interpretations

When preparing a play for performance, the director works closely with the actors, deciding how the lines should be spoken. For example, should the actors sound sincere, jokey or sarcastic? How can costumes, facial expressions and gestures reinforce the effect? Below, you can see how a speech from *The Taming of the Shrew* might be played in two different ways. The speech comes at the end of Act V (V.ii.151) when the unruly Katherine has been "tamed" by her new husband Petruchio. He makes a bet with his friends that he has the most submissive wife, and she speaks of how women should be docile and obey their husbands. Part of the speech is shown on the right.

Of course, there are many different ways to deliver these lines. The interpretations shown below are just two possible approaches. If you were the director, how would you present Katherine's speech?

> *Thy husband is thy lord, thy life, thy keeper,*
> *Thy head, thy sovereign, one that cares for thee,*
> *And for thy maintenance commits his body*
> *To painful labour both by sea and land,*
> *To watch the night in storms, the day in cold,*
> *Whilst thou liest warm at home, secure and safe,*
> *And craves no other tribute at thy hands*
> *But love, fair looks, and true obedience,*
> *Too little payment for so great a debt.*
> *Such duty as the subject owes the prince,*
> *Even such a woman oweth to her husband,*
> *And when she is froward, peevish, sullen, sour,*
> *And not obedient to his honest will,*
> *What is she but a foul contending rebel,*
> *And graceless traitor to her loving lord?*
> *I am ashamed that women are so simple*
> *To offer war where they should kneel for peace,*
> *Or seek for rule, supremacy and sway*
> *When they are bound to love, serve and obey.*

Interpretation 1

In this interpretation, Katherine means what she says. She has fallen in love with Petruchio and has changed. She now accepts different roles for men and women and is prepared to approach her marriage in this way.

- **Tone of voice:** The actress's voice should be sincere and passionate. She should appear to show emotions, such as love for Petruchio, as she speaks. She could use a "ladylike" tone - insistent, but not aggressive.

- **Costume:** An Elizabethan woman's costume would place Katherine in her time and make it easier for the audience to understand her submissiveness.

- **Gestures:** The actress might make heartfelt gestures of love and emphasis, putting her hand on her heart, or wringing her hands. She could also bow her head to look submissive.

- **Delivery:** Speaking her words to Petruchio would show love and obedience to him. Or she could address the other characters on stage, expressing her feelings so as to convince them.

- **The other characters' response:** They should look genuinely affected and moved by her speech. They should appear to be listening carefully and seem impressed.

- **Props:** The director could make use of props to symbolize Katherine's married state. For example, she could display the ring on her finger as a symbol that she belongs to Petruchio. She could even be pregnant.

Interpretation 2

In this interpretation, Katherine is shown as a feminist who thinks women should not have to obey men. Her scornful speech mocks the concept of obedience.

- **Tone of voice:** The actress must show that Katherine actually thinks the opposite of what she is saying. She could exaggerate the submissive tone of the speech and laugh scornfully at the ideas it contains.

- **Costume:** A modern costume would make Katherine's feminism seem realistic - maybe her clothes, for example a business suit, could show how independent she is. But Elizabethan costume might also be effective, showing Katherine as a feminist ahead of her time, surrounded by more traditional views.

- **Gestures:** She could exaggerate the submission by bowing and scraping insincerely to Petruchio, or contradict her own words with rude or aggressive gestures.

- **Delivery:** The speech could be delivered to the audience, showing Katherine mocking the other characters and appealing to the values of the modern theatre-goers.

- **The other characters' response:** The other characters could either be taken in, or they could laugh along with her. Perhaps they could gradually realize what is going on.

- **Props:** Katherine could be reading out a pre-prepared speech which Petruchio hands her. This would show him attempting to prove that she is docile, but failing because he hasn't realized how independent she is.

Performing Shakespeare

Many different kinds of theatre companies put on Shakespeare plays, from small amateur groups to large professional companies. There are dozens of different stages in preparing for a production, such as planning, rehearsing, designing and preparing sets and costumes, advertising the performance and arranging tours. As well as the actors, there are numerous people working behind the scenes to make sure the production goes smoothly.

Before rehearsals begin

There is a lot to do before rehearsals can start. After choosing the play, the director meets the designer to discuss ideas. Actors have to be chosen for the parts, either from within the theatre company, or by holding auditions. It also takes a lot of administration work to book a rehearsal space and a theatre, produce publicity materials such as leaflets, posters, and programs, hire people to work behind the scenes, and arrange for everyone to be paid. The timeline at the bottom of these pages shows how the whole project is planned and arranged.

In rehearsals

Initial readthrough
At the first rehearsal, the members of the company meet in a rehearsal room, and the actors read the play. The director and the designer talk about their plans for the production.
"Calling" and "blocking"
After the initial readthrough, the actors are "called" in groups to work on their scenes with the director. "Blocking" is deciding where on the stage characters should be and which exits and entrances they should use.
"Off book"
As the opening night approaches the actors are "off book" – they are no longer allowed to read from their scripts. They run through scenes, then whole acts, then eventually the whole play.
Technical rehearsal or "tech"
This is held a few days before the first night to check that lighting and other effects are timed properly and that actors are familiar with them.
Dress rehearsal
This takes place shortly before the first performance, with full costume, make-up and lighting.

Actors and a director in a rehearsal for Hamlet. Rehearsals can be exhausting: the director holds up to 20 three-hour sessions a week, though individual actors do not attend every one.

Timeline

This timeline, continued over the next four pages, follows the main stages in the run-up to a play's opening night, from the first decisions to the first night performance.

1 year before

The general manager and artistic director of a theatre choose a play, a director and leading actors.

Budgets are planned. The company looks for funds from government or businesses.

If it is a touring production, theatres are booked in all the towns it will visit.

Nine months

The director assembles the creative team: an assistant director, a designer, a lighting designer, a fight director, a composer, a choreographer and a voice coach.

Three months

The production team is assembled: a stage manager, a deputy stage manager, assistants, and lighting and sound technicians.

The creative team finalizes plans for sets and costumes. Set builders, costume and prop-makers are contracted. Set-building work begins.

The publicity team produces a leaflet and arranges coverage in the press.

Go to **www.usborne-quicklinks.com** for a link to a Web site where you can see set designs from dozens of different productions of Shakespeare plays.

Set design

Working with the director, the designer creates sets and costumes which will convey the atmosphere of a play, and highlight any particular aspects of it that the director wants to emphasize. Sometimes this means designing a set which recreates a particular historical period. The designer may also refer to the text of the play for ideas. For example, in *A Midsummer Night's Dream* Oberon lists several forest flowers, including "wild thyme", "the nodding violet", "luscious woodbine" and "sweet musk-roses". A designer could find out what these flowers look like and recreate them in the set. Or he or she may be asked to design an abstract set, or to use objects and lighting in a symbolic way.

There are also many practical considerations to take into account: the size and shape of the theatre, the technology available, the time allowed for building and, of course, the cost. If it is a touring production, the designer also has to make sure that the set can be dismantled and rebuilt in different theatres.

Two set designs for Shakespeare plays: an abstract design for *A Midsummer Night's Dream*, above, and a more traditional design for *The Tempest*, recreating the shipwreck on the island.

Ten weeks

Casting for remaining parts begins. The director approaches actors or holds auditions. Second auditions, or "recalls", help the director make a final choice.

The designer makes a model of the set to show to the cast on the first day of rehearsal. The stage manager assembles rehearsal costumes and props.

The publicity team sends out press releases to theatre critics inviting them to the first night, and arranges newspaper advertising.

Four to six weeks

Rehearsals begin with the initial readthrough. Then the director works on individual scenes with groups of actors.

The program is written and printed.

The actors meet the administrative staff. The publicity department finds out as much as possible about the actors for press reports. The financial controller arranges their payment.

Three weeks

Actors are called for daily rehearsals.

Actors attend voice classes, fight rehearsals, music rehearsals and costume fittings.

Understudies rehearse with the assistant director. They must learn to give a similar performance to the actor they are "covering" so that they can join the show without unsettling other actors.

Costumes

Costumes can help to set a play in a historical period, whether the play's original setting or a different period. Some productions use costumes from several historical periods. This can say a lot about different characters. For example, a young character like Cordelia in *King Lear* could wear fashionable clothes, while her father, the old king, could wear an old-fashioned uniform or suit to show his authority. Costumes are also used for special effects, such as making an actor look fatter.

How a costume is made

There are several stages involved in making theatrical costumes.

Researching: The designer researches historical periods or concepts, and looks for suitable fabrics.

Designing: The designer shows costume sketches to the creative team and actors, along with swatches (samples) of suggested fabrics.

Final design: When everyone has agreed on the costume designs, the designer draws final versions, and the material is bought.

Making: Following the design, the actors are measured and the costume makers make the costumes.

Fitting: The actors come to be fitted with their costumes. Usually, more than one of each item is made, as the costumes can get dirty during the performances.

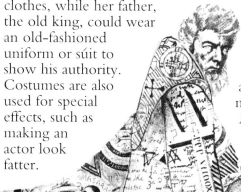

Left: a costume design for Prospero in *The Tempest*.

Above: swatches are needed to see how various fabrics will look under stage lights.

Craftspeople with specialist skills may be needed to put the finishing touches to a costume. This embroiderer is adding a detailed decoration to some cloth.

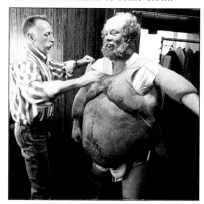

Some costumes involve padding the actor's body. This actor is being fitted with a fat latex "belly" to play Falstaff in *The Merry Wives of Windsor*.

Two weeks before

By now, the actors are running through large chunks of the play "off book" (without referring to the script).

One week

Props are collected by the stage managers, and gradually arrive in the rehearsal rooms. They are incorporated into rehearsals.

A few days

The production team begins the "fit-up" in the theatre. Lights are rigged (put in the right positions) and focused. Computer lighting boards are programmed. The set is put up. Costumes are laid out in the dressing rooms.

The technical rehearsal is held to try out the lighting and set changes and to make sure any machinery, such as a revolving stage, is working.

Many Shakespeare productions still have the actors wearing Elizabethan costumes. Go to **www.usborne-quicklinks.com** for a link to a Web site that has lots of information and tips on recreating Elizabethan dress.

Make-up

For most roles, actors need to wear make-up. It can be used in various ways. Often, it simply highlights ordinary facial features, to make sure the actors' expressions are visible from the very back of the theatre. Or it can be used to change the shade of the skin, or to make actors look older or younger than they are. It can also be used to make actors look ill, injured, evil or supernatural. Normal make-up can be used, but theatre companies generally use special stage make-up.

A make-up table in a theatre dressing-room. The mirror is brightly lit and the table is covered with a huge range of stage make-up.

This picture shows how stage make-up can make a young actor look old. On the right-hand side, you can see what the actor really looks like.

Deep wrinkles are made with lines of dark make-up.

Eyebrows are thickened with brown make-up.

Shadows are drawn under the eyes.

False hair is used to make a beard and sideburns, which are glued to the actor's face.

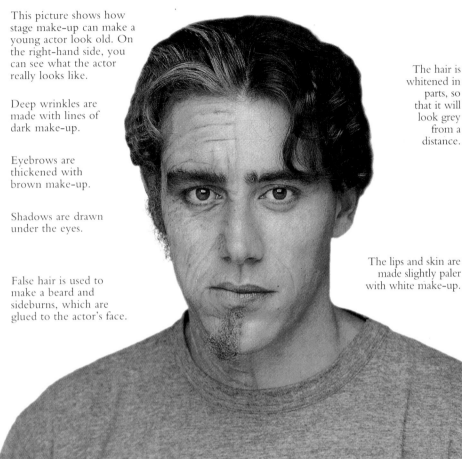

The hair is whitened in parts, so that it will look grey from a distance.

The lips and skin are made slightly paler with white make-up.

Here, an actress has her eye make-up applied by the make-up artist. In smaller theatre companies, the actors often put on their own make-up. Most large companies, though, employ a professional make-up artist.

What beard were I best to play it in? *A Midsummer Night's Dream, I.ii.83-84*

The day before

The dress rehearsal is held and the director gives "notes" (comments) on the performance to let the company know how it went.

The day of the first performance

Final alterations are made to the lighting, set and costumes.

The director gives a few final notes and reminders and encourages the company for the big night ahead.

5.30pm

All technical crew must be at the theatre by this time.

6.30pm

Actors go to their dressing rooms: make-up is put on and they change into costume.

6.55pm

35 minutes before curtain up is called "the half". All the actors must be in the theatre by now. If an actor hasn't arrived, an understudy gets ready to go on instead.

7.25pm

Five minutes before the performance starts is called "beginners". The opening actors must be ready to go on.

7.30pm

The performance starts.

Shakespeare as inspiration

Shakespeare's contribution to the arts goes far beyond his own work. His influence has spread all over the world and to all forms of art. There have been many film and television productions of his plays, and his plots, characters and poetry have caught the imagination of other artists, from composers to cartoonists, and inspired them to create their own works of art.

Many artists have painted characters or scenes from Shakespeare's plays. This painting, *The Death of Ophelia*, by the English artist John Everett Millais, shows Ophelia drowning, as described in Act IV, Scene vii of *Hamlet*.

Shakespeare on film

Shakespeare's works were made into some of the earliest silent films, soon after the invention of cinema. Since then the plays have often been adapted to suit the big screen. The English actor Laurence Olivier directed a very patriotic film of *Henry V* in 1944 during the Second World War. He cut out many of the lines from the play about the horror of war. The Japanese director Akira Kurosawa moved even further from the original texts for his film versions of *Macbeth* (called *The Throne of Blood*) and *King Lear* (called *Ran*), setting them in historical Japan. In *Ran*, for example, the King has sons, not daughters, and a wife, unlike Shakespeare's King Lear.

A puppet of the character Malvolio, from a Russian animated film of *Twelfth Night* which was made for television.

Left: a poster advertising Akira Kurosawa's *Ran*, a Japanese film version of *King Lear*.

In the 1960s, the Italian director Franco Zeffirelli filmed some of the plays in the Italian cities where Shakespeare set them. In his *Romeo and Juliet* the lovers are seen on a real balcony in Verona, and *The Taming of the Shrew* was filmed around Padua. More recently, Kenneth Branagh has made popular Shakespeare films including *Henry V* (1990), *Much Ado About Nothing* (1993), *Hamlet* (1996) and *Love's Labour's Lost* (2000).

Go to **www.usborne-quicklinks.com** for a link to a Web site where you can look at paintings inspired by Shakespeare.

Shakespearean spin-offs

Shakespeare's plays have often been the starting point for original work by other playwrights. For example, Tom Stoppard's *Rosencrantz and Guildenstern are Dead* (1966) focuses on the lives of these two minor characters from *Hamlet*, telling the story from their point of view. Their conversations are interspersed with scenes and events from the original play.

The opera singer Placido Domingo starring in Verdi's *Otello*, a version of *Othello*.

Right:
The Reduced Shakespeare Company performs a comedy version of the complete works of Shakespeare in only 97 minutes. Each play is recreated in a different style: for example, *Othello* is performed as a rap song.

Ballets, operas and musicals have also been based on Shakespeare's works. Some, like Verdi's operas *Macbeth* (1865) and *Otello* (1887) are based closely on the original plays, but others are looser adaptations. Leonard Bernstein's *West Side Story* (1957) is a musical based on *Romeo and Juliet*. It is set in New York among two rival teenage gangs, the Jets (Polish immigrants) and the Sharks (Puerto Ricans), who correspond to the two feuding families in the play. *Return to the Forbidden Planet* (1990) is a science fiction musical based loosely on *The Tempest*, with popular songs from the 20th century mixed in. It is set on a fictitious planet where Dr. Prospero has been banished by his ex-wife. Ariel is a robot, and Caliban takes the form of several monsters that spring from Dr. Prospero's evil imagination.

A scene from *West Side Story*, a modern musical by Leonard Bernstein based on Shakespeare's *Romeo and Juliet*.

How far that little candle throws his beams The Merchant of Venice, V.i.90

Plots of Shakespeare's plays

❧ All's Well That Ends Well ❧

Helena secretly loves Bertram, the young Count of Roussillon, who is summoned to serve at the court of the King of France in Paris. The King is dying, and Helena, whose father was a great doctor, follows Bertram to Paris and cures the King, using secret prescriptions prepared by her father before he died. As a reward, the King tells her she may choose a husband from his court. She chooses Bertram.

Unwillingly, Bertram marries her, but immediately goes to the wars in Florence with his friend Parolles. He sends Helena a letter saying he will not come back to her unless she can remove the ring from his finger and have his child. He thinks these things will never happen.

On a pilgrimage, Helena visits Florence, staying with a widow. She finds that Bertram is courting the widow's daughter Diana. Sending Bertram news that she is dead, she arranges to stand in for Diana and sleep with Bertram. He gives her his ring, thinking she is Diana, and she gives him a ring she got from the King.

Bertram visits his mother's house, where the King is staying. Seeing his ring, the King demands an explanation from Bertram. At last, Helena arrives and explains everything, and the two are united.

❧ Antony and Cleopatra ❧

Mark Antony, a great soldier and, together with Octavius Caesar and Lepidus, one of the three rulers of Rome, is in Egypt, in love with its glamorous Queen, Cleopatra. The death of his wife Fulvia and other events force him to return to Rome, where he promises to attend to his duties. He marries Caesar's sister Octavia to cement his friendship with Caesar, but cannot resist returning to Cleopatra. This leads to war. Antony's forces are defeated by Rome, and he blames Cleopatra for his failure. Terrified, she sends him news that she is dead and hides in a monument. Hearing the news, Antony stabs himself, and is taken, dying, to Cleopatra. After his death, refusing to give herself up to Rome, Cleopatra kills herself with a bite from a poisonous snake.

❧ As You Like It ❧

Oliver has ignored his father's will and withheld his brother Orlando's inheritance. He plans for Orlando to be killed in a wrestling match at court, where Duke Senior has been deposed and banished to the forest by his brother Duke Frederick. But Orlando wins the match, and also falls in love with Rosalind, Duke Senior's daughter. Duke Frederick banishes Orlando when he finds out that his father was one of his enemies, and also banishes Rosalind. Celia, Duke Frederick's daughter, promises to go with her. They decide to join Duke Senior in the Forest of Arden.

Disguised as brother and sister, Ganymede and Aliena, the women arrive at the forest, where they find Orlando, who is also hiding there, and Duke Senior and his party. Oliver comes to kill Orlando, but repents when Orlando saves him from a lion. He falls in love with "Aliena", or Celia, and wedding plans are made for the next day. "Ganymede" promises Orlando that he will be able to marry Rosalind at the same time. Rosalind also helps a shepherd, Corin, to win over his beloved Phoebe.

During celebrations, news arrives that Duke Frederick has repented and returned the dukedom to Duke Senior.

❧ The Comedy of Errors ❧

Egeon, an old man from Syracuse, is arrested in Ephesus, which is at war with Syracuse. He explains that he and his wife had twins, both called Antipholus. They had twin slaves, both called Dromio. The wife, one son and one slave were separated from the others in a shipwreck. The other son and slave set off to look for them and have now disappeared. Now the old man is searching for his family.

The Duke gives Egeon a day to pay a ransom, or be executed. It turns out that the shipwrecked Antipholus and Dromio have been living in Syracuse, while the other two have arrived there that day. Everyone gets the twins mixed up, with comic results. Finally, as Egeon is led to his execution, both sons appear together, everything is explained, and Egeon is pardoned and freed. The abbess of the convent turns out to be Egeon's wife, Emilia.

❧ Coriolanus ❧

The great Roman soldier Caius Marcius defeats the Volscians, and after capturing the town of Corioli he is awarded the name Coriolanus. He is to be made a consul (chief magistrate) but, because he is proud and snobbish and refuses to show the crowd his war wounds in the traditional way, he becomes unpopular and is banished.

Coriolanus goes to join his old enemy, the Volscian general Aufidius, and leads a Volscian army to attack Rome in revenge. At the walls of the city, his old friends cannot persuade him to spare Rome from destruction. But when his mother, Volumnia, makes a rhetorical speech, Coriolanus gives in and makes a treaty. He returns to Aufidius, who furiously accuses him of betrayal, and kills him in front of an angry crowd.

❧ Cymbeline ❧

Imogen, daughter of King Cymbeline of Britain, has secretly married Posthumus. Her stepmother, the queen, who had wanted her to marry her son Cloten, tells the King about Imogen's marriage, and he banishes Posthumus. In Italy, Posthumus makes a bet that Iachimo will not be able to seduce Imogen. Iachimo goes to Britain and hides in Imogen's room. He reports details of her appearance to Posthumus, who is convinced that she has been unfaithful. Posthumus orders his servant Pisanio to kill Imogen for her supposed infidelity, but instead Pisanio helps her to escape, disguised as a boy, Fidele.

"Fidele" becomes a page to Belarius and to Cymbeline's two long-lost sons, Guiderius and Arviragus, in Wales. She falls ill and the brothers think "he" is dead, but later she wakes, finds Cloten's headless body, and mistakes it for Posthumus. Then "Fidele" becomes a servant to Lucius, a general in the Roman army invading Britain. Britain defeats the Romans, helped by Posthumus, Belarius and Cymbeline's sons. At Lucius's request, "Fidele" is spared by Cymbeline. "He" asks that Iachimo tell his story. The truth is revealed to Posthumus, and Imogen and her two long-lost brothers reveal who they are.

❦ Hamlet ❦

Hamlet, Prince of Denmark, sees his dead father's ghost, who tells him that he was murdered by his brother Claudius, and urges him to take revenge. Claudius is now king and has married Hamlet's mother, Queen Gertrude. Hamlet decides to pretend to be insane while he works out what to do. He rejects his old girlfriend Ophelia, the daughter of Polonius, a lord. He arranges a play to be put on, in which a king is murdered by his nephew. Claudius calls off the performance, seeming guilty or worried. Hamlet talks to his mother in her bedroom, and stabs through a curtain behind which Polonius is hiding, killing him. Claudius sends Hamlet to England with Rosencrantz and Guildenstern, with instructions for them to kill him, but Hamlet escapes and returns to Denmark.

During his absence, Ophelia has gone insane with grief and drowned. Her brother Laertes has returned from France and encounters Hamlet in the graveyard where Ophelia is to be buried. Claudius arranges a duel, giving Laertes a poisoned sword with which to fight Hamlet, also providing a cup of poison for Hamlet to drink. But the swords get mixed up, both Laertes and Hamlet are fatally wounded, and Gertrude accidentally drinks the poison. Before dying, Hamlet manages at last to kill Claudius with the poisoned sword.

❦ Henry IV, Part 1 ❦

Henry Percy, nicknamed Hotspur, a brave soldier and originally an ally of Henry IV, decides to raise a rebel army to depose the King.

Meanwhile the King's son, Prince Henry, known as Hal, is having fun with his drinking friends, Falstaff and Poins. Falstaff and other thieves carry out a highway robbery. In disguise, Hal and Poins ambush them and steal the money they have stolen. Later, Falstaff lies about his courage in seeing off these "attackers".

Hal is summoned by his father to fight Hotspur's rebel army. Falstaff is a coward in battle, but Hal proves himself by killing Hotspur. The King's troops are victorious and plans are made to defeat the remaining rebels.

❦ Henry IV, Part 2 ❦

When Lord Northumberland learns that his son, Hotspur, has been killed in battle, he decides, with the Archbishop of York, to raise another rebel army against the King.

Falstaff, the debauched friend of the King's son, Prince Hal, is arrested for not paying his debts in a tavern, but the charges are later dropped. Hal, disguised as a waiter, joins Falstaff in the tavern and plays tricks on him.

Northumberland, influenced by his wife and daughter-in-law, decides not to join York and Lord Hastings in fighting the King after all. He flees to Scotland. Hal and Falstaff are summoned to battle. Falstaff becomes a recruiting officer.

At Gaultree, Prince John of Lancaster persuades York and Hastings to disband their armies on condition that they will be pardoned, but when they surrender, they are immediately sentenced to death.

The King, dying in his bed, bemoans Hal's delinquent conduct. Hal comes to his bedside and promises him that he has reformed. The King dies and Hal is crowned Henry V.

Henry V is greeted by his old friend Falstaff, but pretends not to know him and banishes him.

❦ Henry V ❦

Henry, with the support of his nobles, decides to reclaim the French throne. Ambassadors from France arrive at Court and rudely warn Henry against carrying out his plans, but Henry responds by declaring war on France.

Falstaff, Henry's former friend (see *Henry IV, Parts 1* and *2*), dies broken-hearted that Henry has rejected him.

English troops lay siege to the town of Harfleur, which soon surrenders. The French King orders a massive assault by French troops. The English prepare for battle. The English troops are desperately outnumbered at Agincourt but Henry urges them to fight bravely with a rallying battle cry.

The English are victorious. A peace treaty is signed and preparations begin for the marriage of Henry to the French Princess, Katherine.

❦ Henry VI, Part 1 ❦

This play begins with Henry V's funeral and deals with rebellions in France by supporters of Henry VI, the Lancastrian King of England.

In France, the English Lord Talbot proves himself to be a hero against the French, who are helped by a witch-like young woman called Joan La Pucelle (Joan of Arc).

In England, several factions argue bitterly, especially Richard Plantagenet, Duke of York, and the Duke of Somerset.

The French are eventually defeated in Rouen. Henry VI divides the English forces between the command of the rivals York and Somerset. Both refuse to go to the aid of Talbot, who dies in battle. After further English victories, a peace treaty is arranged. Joan is burned as a witch, and the Earl of Suffolk arranges a marriage between Henry VI and Margaret of Anjou, declaring he will use his influence to control King, Queen and kingdom.

❦ Henry VI, Part 2 ❦

The Duke of Gloucester is angry about Henry VI's marriage contract to Margaret of Anjou, which gives back captured French land to her father. Plotting by other nobles leads to Gloucester's arrest for treason, and his murder. Suffolk is banished for his part in Gloucester's death, and murdered by pirates. The Duke of York, who plans to seize the throne, stirs up a rebellion by Jack Cade, who is eventually killed. Finally, York and Somerset (a Lancastrian) fight at Saint Albans. Somerset is killed and York's position is strengthened.

❦ Henry VI, Part 3 ❦

Henry VI tries to make peace with the Duke of York by making him heir to the throne, disinheriting his own son. Queen Margaret is furious and has York's youngest son killed. Civil war breaks out. York is killed but Henry is captured and York's eldest son, Edward, becomes king. Margaret's son is killed by Edward and his brothers, George, Duke of Clarence, and Richard. Henry, imprisoned in the tower, is murdered by the ruthlessly ambitious Richard.

❧ Henry VIII ❧

England has fallen under the influence of the Catholic Cardinal Wolsey. On the advice of Wolsey, King Henry has Buckingham arrested for treason.

In a council meeting, the Queen, Katherine speaks for the people against the unjust taxes raised by Wolsey. The King orders Wolsey to abandon the taxes.

In a London street scene, two gentlemen remark on how Buckingham is beloved by the people and Wolsey hated. Buckingham passes on his way to execution, forgiving his enemies.

Henry decides to divorce Katherine, on the grounds that the marriage is illegal. Katherine reluctantly agrees, but is deeply humiliated by Wolsey, who wants the divorce for his own ambitious reasons.

Wolsey loses his influence and falls from power as Henry discovers the extent of his greed, and because of his opposition to Henry's marriage to the Protestant Anne Bullen (Anne Boleyn). Henry marries Anne, and their child Elizabeth (later to be Elizabeth I) is christened by the new Protestant archbishop, Thomas Cranmer.

❧ Julius Caesar ❧

Julius Caesar, leader of Rome's armies, has arrived home from successful campaigns in Spain. Certain Romans, particularly Cassius and Casca, distrust him and think he wants too much power. They convince his friend Brutus that Caesar is dangerous, and form a conspiracy against him. They murder Caesar in the Senate (parliament). Brutus asks Antony, Caesar's supporter, to join them, and grants Antony his request to make a speech to the people. Antony secretly plans to revenge Caesar's death.

In his speech over Caesar's body, Antony stirs the crowd into a fury. He then unites with Octavius, Caesar's nephew, and Lepidus against the armies of Brutus and Cassius. Without the full support of the people, and guilty about Caesar's death, Brutus quarrels with Cassius, and is also upset by the death of his wife. After being defeated in the battle of Philippi, Brutus and Cassius kill themselves.

❧ King John ❧

Supported by King Philip of France, Arthur, nephew of the English King, John, makes a claim on the English throne. In response, John declares war on France. A peace settlement is made between Philip and John, but is soon broken when John is excommunicated by the Pope, and Philip, under threat of excommunication, resumes hostilities against England.

Meanwhile, John has captured Arthur and plans to have him killed. Arthur is spared, but dies while trying to escape. His body is found by a group of nobles, who defect to the invading French army. John is poisoned by a monk and dies. His son, Henry, is recognized as king and the French make offers of peace.

❧ King Lear ❧

King Lear of Britain decides to divide his land between his three daughters, according to how much they love him. Goneril and Regan make elaborate speeches of affection, and are awarded land, but Cordelia, the youngest, although she loves him too, refuses to join in with what she sees as their insincerity. She says she loves her father only as much as is fitting. Furiously, Lear casts her out, and she leaves with her suitor, the King of France. Lear goes to live first with Goneril, then Regan, but they treat him harshly and eventually he is thrown out in a storm, with his fool.

Meanwhile, Edmund, the bastard son of the Earl of Gloucester, has turned his father against his legitimate son Edgar. Edmund becomes the lover of both Goneril and Regan, while Edgar flees, disguised as a crazy beggar. Gloucester expresses pity for Lear and is suspected of supporting the French, who have landed at Dover to save Lear. Gloucester has his eyes put out by Cornwall, Regan's husband, and is cared for by Edgar in disguise.

Jealous over Edmund, Goneril poisons Regan and kills herself. Lear, having gone mad, is taken to Dover where he is reconciled with Cordelia. The English, led by Edmund and Cornwall, defeat the French, and Lear and Cordelia are imprisoned. Edgar kills Edmund in a duel, but Cordelia is hanged, and Lear dies of grief.

❧ Love's Labour's Lost ❧

The King of Navarre and his three courtiers, Longaville, Maine and Berowne, take an oath to devote themselves to studying, and to avoid women, for three years. The Princess of France arrives on a visit with her three ladies. The King decides to house them in his palace grounds. He falls in love with the Princess, and his courtiers with her ladies. The ladies tease the young men, who woo them while trying to hide their infatuations from each other.

Meanwhile, a visiting Spaniard, Armado, is in love with a country girl, Jacquenetta. The King discovers Armado's love and that of the courtiers. Eventually, Berowne argues that they should all abandon their three-year abstinence and study love. However, a pageant held to celebrate is interrupted by news that the Princess's father, the King of France, has died, making her the queen. The ladies must leave, so they impose a year's wait on their lovers.

❧ Macbeth ❧

Returning triumphant from battle, Macbeth and Banquo encounter three witches on a heath, who predict that Macbeth shall be Thane of Cawdor, and subsequently King of Scotland, and that Banquo shall be a father of kings. Soon Macbeth hears that he has been made Thane of Cawdor. Spurred on by the prophecy and by his ambitious wife Lady Macbeth, Macbeth murders King Duncan, who is visiting his castle at Dunsinane. Duncan's sons Malcolm and Donalbain flee in terror, and Macbeth is crowned king.

Macbeth has Banquo killed, but Banquo's son Fleance escapes. Macbeth revisits the witches and is told that he should beware Macduff, that he can be harmed by no man born of woman, and that he is safe until Birnam Wood comes to Dunsinane. Macbeth has Macduff's wife and children killed, while his own wife goes mad and dies. Malcolm brings an army to attack Dunsinane, using leaves from Birnam Wood as camouflage, and Macduff, who was not born, but cut from his mother's body, kills Macbeth. Malcolm is proclaimed king.

Go to **www.usborne-quicklinks.com** for a link to a Web site where you'll find excellent plot summaries and guides to the characters and themes of all Shakespeare's plays.

❀ Measure for Measure ❀

The Duke of Vienna has decided to hand over power to his deputy, Angelo. Angelo sentences a young man, Claudio, to death for getting his fiancée, Juliet, pregnant. The Duke appears disguised as a friar to watch over Angelo's rule.

Claudio's sister, Isabella, is about to become a nun. She is persuaded to plead with Angelo for mercy. Angelo agrees to free Claudio if she will sleep with him. Isabella refuses. The "friar" finds out about this and persuades Mariana, Angelo's ex-fiancée, to take Isabella's place in the dark, so that she sleeps with Angelo. Angelo doesn't notice the swap, but breaks his promise and orders Claudio's death. The Duke secretly saves Claudio's life.

In the final scene, the "friar" reveals his true identity as the Duke. Angelo is ordered to marry Mariana, and is then condemned to death. Mariana and Isabella plead for mercy for Angelo and he is pardoned. Claudio prepares to marry Juliet, and the Duke proposes to Isabella.

❀ The Merchant of Venice ❀

Bassanio asks his friend Antonio, a rich merchant, for a loan to help him woo Portia. Antonio's wealth is all invested in merchant ships, so he goes to the Jewish money-lender, Shylock. Shylock, angry that Antonio has insulted him in the past, lends the money on condition that if it is not returned within three months, he will cut off a pound of Antonio's flesh.

Portia's father's will requires her suitors to choose from gold, silver and lead caskets. The lead casket entitles the chooser to marry her. Bassanio chooses it, and marries Portia, and his friend Gratiano marries her maid Nerissa. But then news arrives that Antonio's ships are missing, so he cannot repay the debt. Portia and Nerissa, disguised as a lawyer and his clerk, go to the court to save Antonio. Portia argues that although Shylock may take Antonio's flesh, he must not spill any blood. Shylock cannot do this, and is ordered to give half his wealth to Antonio. Under duress, he agrees to become a Christian. Finally, news comes that Antonio's ships are safe after all.

❀ The Merry Wives of Windsor ❀

Falstaff (a comic rogue who also appears in *Henry IV*) plans to seduce two married women, Mrs. Ford and Mrs. Page. Two of his followers, Nym and Pistol, who have been dismissed, warn the ladies' husbands. When Falstaff sends the women identical love letters, they decide to punish him.

Falstaff is invited to visit Mrs. Ford, and the women torment him, first hiding him in a basket of dirty laundry when the suspicious Mr. Ford arrives. Later they disguise him as "the old woman of Brainford", whom Mr. Ford beats out of the house. Finally, the women, aided by their husbands, arrange a rendezvous in the woods, where Falstaff is attacked by "fairies" (various friends in disguise).

Meanwhile, three suitors are pursuing Mrs. Page's daughter Anne. At the final meeting in the woods, two of them, Slender and Caius, are tricked, while Anne runs off and marries her preferred suitor, the handsome Fenton. The play ends in forgiveness as everyone is invited to a party at the Fords' house.

❀ A Midsummer Night's Dream ❀

Hermia loves Lysander, but is under orders from her father Egeus and the Duke, Theseus, to marry Demetrius. She and Lysander escape to the forest, followed by Demetrius, who in turn is pursued by Helena, who loves him.

Oberon, king of the fairies, has fallen out with his wife Titania, and tells his servant Puck to squeeze love-juice on her eyes so that she falls in love with the first person she sees. He also orders Puck to use the love-juice to sort out the young lovers' problems, but this goes wrong, and both men end up chasing Helena. Meanwhile, Titania has fallen in love with Bottom, a weaver who has been given an ass's head by Puck. Oberon and Titania resolve their quarrel, and Puck uses magic to restore the four lovers to happy couples. Egeus and the Duke arrive, and the runaways are forgiven. The weddings of Hermia and Lysander and Helena and Demetrius take place, along with the Duke's own wedding to Hippolyta. Bottom and his fellow workmen perform a play.

❀ Much Ado About Nothing ❀

After military campaigns, Don Pedro, the Prince of Aragon, arrives at the house of Leonato with his men, including Benedick, Claudio, and the Prince's brother Don John. Claudio falls in love with Hero, Leonato's daughter, while Benedick and Beatrice, Leonato's niece, exchange witty insults and swear they will never marry, although their friends insist that they are falling in love with each other. Don Pedro arranges for Claudio to marry Hero, but Don John tricks him into believing Hero has been unfaithful to him. On the wedding day, Claudio angrily denounces Hero and she faints and appears to have died. Benedick challenges Claudio to a duel, saying he is doing it for Beatrice. Then Don John's plot is uncovered by the comic local constables, Dogberry and Verges. Claudio tries to make amends for what has happened, and is asked to marry a cousin of Hero's, who, when she is unveiled, turns out to be Hero herself, recovered from her faint. Benedick and Beatrice finally make wedding plans too, and the play ends in a joyful dance.

❀ Othello ❀

Othello, a black Venetian general, has secretly married Desdemona, who is white. Her father is angry, but Othello justifies himself and is asked to sail to Cyprus to defend it against the Turks.

Iago, Othello's ensign (a kind of army officer), is jealous that the younger Cassio has been promoted above him. He gets Cassio drunk and involves him in a fight. Demoted by Othello, Cassio asks Desdemona to plead with Othello for him, which she does. Iago suggests to Othello that Desdemona and Cassio are secret lovers. Iago also obtains Desdemona's handkerchief, a present from Othello, through his wife Emilia who is Desdemona's waiting lady, and plants it on Cassio. Othello is driven to distraction, unable to bear the thought that Desdemona has deceived him, and afraid that she prefers Cassio because he is white. Eventually Othello murders Desdemona. Too late, Emilia reveals Iago's deception to Othello, who commits suicide.

Pericles

Pericles, Prince of Tyre, is forced to leave Antioch when he discovers the King's secret incest. He is shipwrecked off Pentapolis, where he enters a jousting competition and wins the hand of Thaisa, the King of Pentapolis's daughter. Pericles and Thaisa set sail to return to Tyre. En route, Thaisa apparently dies in childbirth. Her body is buried at sea, but her coffin is washed ashore at Ephesus where a doctor revives her. Thaisa, believing her husband to have drowned, enters a convent dedicated to the goddess Diana.

Fearing she will not survive the voyage, Pericles leaves his baby daughter, Marina, at Tarsus in the care of its governor Cleon and his wife, Dionyza. As Marina grows into a beautiful young woman, Dionyza grows jealous for her own, plainer daughter, so orders Marina's murder, telling Pericles his daughter has died naturally. Marina escapes death when she is captured by pirates, taken to Mytilene and sold to a brothel. Here, she narrowly avoids becoming a prostitute, and meets the governor of Mytilene, Lysimachus. The grieving Pericles arrives at Mytilene where he is reunited with his daughter. Following instructions from a dream, Pericles and Marina visit the temple of Diana in Ephesus. They find Thaisa, the family is reunited, and Marina is engaged to Lysimachus.

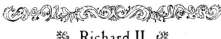

Richard II

Henry Bolingbroke (the King's cousin) and Thomas Mowbray are banished by Richard II because they are arguing. Bolingbroke's father, old John of Gaunt, is very upset at his son's exile.

Richard learns of a rebellion in Ireland, and plans to raise money for an Irish expedition. The dying Gaunt summons Richard and tries to warn him of his extravagance. Richard refuses to listen and on Gaunt's death confiscates his estates. Noblemen, concerned at Richard's actions, decide to support Bolingbroke, who returns to England. Returning from Ireland, Richard surrenders the crown to Bolingbroke, and is sent to Pomfret Castle. He is murdered by Sir Pierce Exton, a loyal subject of Bolingbroke.

Richard III

Richard, brother of King Edward IV, tells the King that their brother George, Duke of Clarence, is plotting treason. Clarence is arrested, and Richard has him killed. Edward, who has been ill, now dies. Richard confines Edward's two young sons to the Tower. Edward's widow Elizabeth mistrusts Richard, who executes her brother and another of her sons.

Richard promises Buckingham an earldom, and with his help is declared king. He arranges the murder of the two princes. Buckingham asks Richard for his earldom but is refused. He joins Richard's enemies, but is captured and executed.

Henry Tudor, Earl of Richmond, arrives in England with an army, meeting Richard at Bosworth. The night before the battle, both men see the ghosts of Richard's victims, who torment Richard but spur Richmond on. The next day, Richmond kills Richard and is declared Henry VII.

Romeo and Juliet

The two leading families of Verona, the Capulets and the Montagues, are feuding. Romeo, a Montague, falls in love with Juliet, a Capulet, at a ball which he attends in disguise. That night, he waits under her window and hears her speak of her love for him. He declares his love for her. They marry in secret the next day, helped by Friar Laurence.

Tybalt, a Capulet, quarrels with and kills Romeo's friend Mercutio. Romeo, arriving on the scene, kills Tybalt. He is banished, and after spending the night with Juliet, goes to Mantua. Meanwhile, Juliet's father wants her to marry Paris. The friar tells Juliet to agree to this, but arranges for her to take a potion which will make her seem dead for two days. He plans to warn Romeo, who will rescue her from her tomb, but the message to Romeo goes astray. Romeo, hearing that Juliet is dead, comes to the tomb, and kills Paris who is there too. Then he kisses Juliet, takes poison and dies. Juliet awakens and, seeing what has happened, stabs herself. On discovery of the tragedy, the two families are finally persuaded to end their quarrel.

The Taming of the Shrew

Baptista, a gentleman of Padua, will not let his daughter Bianca marry until her older, bad-tempered sister Katherine, the "shrew", is married. Petruchio offers to marry Katherine to help his friend Hortensio to woo Bianca, and also to gain Katherine's wealth. He then goes about "taming" her. Whenever she is rude to him, he teases her back. He arrives late for their wedding, wearing ridiculous clothes. At his house, he stops her from eating or sleeping by saying he has no food or furniture good enough for her. Meanwhile, another suitor, Lucentio, wins Bianca, and Hortensio has to marry a widow. At the feast to celebrate the weddings, Petruchio bets that his wife is the most docile. He wins the bet when Katherine makes a speech about how women should be submissive to their husbands.

The Tempest

Prospero, the Duke of Milan, deposed by his brother Antonio and cast out to sea with his baby daughter Miranda, has been marooned on a remote island. With his knowledge of magic, he has liberated the island from the rule of the witch Sycorax and freed certain spirits, which are now in his service. The action begins twelve years later, when Prospero uses his magic to shipwreck Antonio, his accomplice Alonso, King of Naples, and Alonso's son Ferdinand and brother Sebastian on the island.

On Prospero's orders, the spirit Ariel leads Ferdinand to Miranda. They fall in love. Prospero sets Ferdinand some tests to prove he is worthy of his daughter. Meanwhile, Antonio, Alonso and Sebastian are tormented by Ariel's magic tricks.

Prospero consents to the marriage of Miranda and Ferdinand and conjures up a masque to entertain them. Prospero sends Ariel to fetch Alonso, Antonio and Sebastian. They recognize him and he forgives them.

In a comic subplot, Prospero's half-human slave, Caliban, and Trinculo and Stephano, two drunken survivors of the shipwreck, plan to take over the island, but are thwarted by Prospero's magic and their own greed and stupidity.

❧ Timon of Athens ❧

The nobleman Timon has bankrupted himself by being too generous. He turns to his rich friends for help, but all refuse. Bitterly, he invites them to a banquet where he serves only hot water. Then he leaves Athens and goes to live a wild, lonely life in a cave. He finds a hoard of gold while digging for roots, but he is no longer interested in money. When his friends finally ask him to return to Athens, he tells them to hang themselves. At the end his tomb is found with an epitaph declaring his hatred of other people.

❧ Titus Andronicus ❧

Titus, a Roman general, returns to Rome after fighting the Goths, with Tamora, Queen of the Goths, and her sons as captives. Tamora's eldest son is sacrificed. Titus's daughter Lavinia is to marry the Emperor, Saturninus, but he marries Tamora instead. Tamora and her lover, Aaron, plot revenge on Titus and her sons rape Lavinia, cut off her hands and tongue, and set up Titus's sons as murderers. Aaron, holding them prisoner, tells Titus his sons will be freed if he cuts off his hand. Titus does this, but the hand is returned with his sons' heads.

Titus's last son, Lucius, captures Aaron, while Tamora and her sons visit Titus in disguise. He recognizes them, kills the sons, cooks their flesh in a pie and serves it to Tamora, then kills her too. Titus is killed by Saturninus, and Saturninus by Lucius.

❧ Troilus and Cressida ❧

The play is set during the Trojan War. Troilus, a Trojan, is in love with Cressida, whose father has deserted to the Greeks. Cressida's uncle Pandarus brings the lovers together, and they swear to be faithful to each other. But as part of a prisoner swap, Cressida is handed over to the Greeks. Troilus promises to visit her secretly, but sees her making a date with a Greek, Diomedes. He vows to kill Diomedes the next day, but fails to do so. This story is set against battles between the Trojans and the Greeks and internal in-fighting. The play ends with the murder of the Trojan Prince, Hector.

❧ Twelfth Night ❧

Viola has been shipwrecked off Illyria. Brought ashore, she disguises herself as a boy, Cesario, and works as a page for the Duke, Orsino. Orsino sends "him" with messages of love for Olivia, who has so far rejected him, but Olivia falls in love with "Cesario", and Viola falls in love with Orsino.

Meanwhile, Viola's twin brother, Sebastian, has been rescued by Antonio, a sea captain. Antonio mistakes the disguised Viola for Sebastian, and asks her for some money he had entrusted to Sebastian, which he needs to pay off a debt. She cannot provide it, so Antonio is taken to prison. Olivia sees Sebastian, mistakes him for "Cesario", and marries him. Antonio is brought before Orsino. Seeing Cesario again, Antonio still thinks "he" is Sebastian, while Olivia claims she has married "him". At last, Sebastian arrives and the chaos is resolved. When Viola puts on her woman's clothes, Orsino falls in love with her and marries her.

In the farcical sub-plot, Olivia's pompous steward Malvolio is tricked into thinking Olivia loves him by various members of her household.

❧ The Two Gentlemen of Verona ❧

Valentine sets out on his travels and, in Milan, falls in love with Silvia, the Duke's daughter. His friend Proteus leaves for Milan too, vowing to be faithful to his beloved, Julia. But he too falls for Silvia. He tells the Duke that Valentine plans to run off with Silvia. Valentine is exiled, becoming leader of a band of thieves, while Proteus courts Silvia.

Julia decides to follow Proteus. She comes to Milan disguised as a boy, and becomes Proteus's page. Silvia, who prefers Valentine, leaves Milan to follow him and is captured by outlaws. Proteus rescues her and tries to rape her. Valentine appears, and Proteus seems so sorry that Valentine "gives" Silvia to him. Julia, still disguised as a page, faints. At last Proteus recognizes her and rediscovers his love for her. The Duke arrives with Thurio, whom he wants Silvia to marry, but he is so impressed by Valentine that he pardons the outlaws and says Silvia may marry Valentine instead.

❧ The Two Noble Kinsmen ❧

Theseus, Duke of Athens, declares war on the Duke of Thebes. Theseus is victorious. Among the prisoners taken are Palamon and Arcite, who are kinsmen (related to each other). While in prison they spy on Emilia, Theseus's sister-in-law, and fall in love with her. They quarrel over who should woo her and swear to fight a duel if they are released.

Arcite is freed and banished from Athens, but he dons a disguise and becomes Emilia's courtier. Meanwhile, Palamon escapes. The friends meet to fight their duel but are discovered by Theseus who condemns them to death. His wife and Emilia plead for mercy. He decrees they must fight another duel. The winner will marry Emilia but the loser will be executed. Arcite wins but is thrown from his horse and dies, bequeathing Emilia to Palamon.

❧ The Winter's Tale ❧

Leontes, King of Sicily, is convinced that his guest, Polixenes, King of Bohemia, has had an affair with his wife, Hermione. He tries to poison Polixenes but he escapes to Bohemia. Hermione is sent to prison, and gives birth to a daughter. Leontes orders a lord, Antigonus, to take the baby and abandon her in the wilderness.

An oracle (holy prophecy) declares Hermione's innocence. Leontes ignores this, but when his small son Mamillius dies suddenly, he repents. Paulina, Antigonus's wife, reports Hermione's death. Leontes is grief-stricken. Meanwhile, Antigonus and the baby arrive on the Bohemian coast. Antigonus is eaten by a bear, but the baby is found and brought up by a shepherd, who names her Perdita.

Sixteen years pass. In Bohemia, Florizel, Polixenes' son, and Perdita have fallen in love. They flee to Sicily to avoid Polixenes, who has forbidden his son to marry a shepherdess. Here Perdita's true identity is revealed and she is joyfully received by Leontes, her father. Polixenes, who has followed the couple, now gives them his blessing. They all go to see a statue of Hermione. The statue proves to be the real Hermione who is alive and has been cared for by Paulina.

Who's who in the world of Shakespeare

This is a guide to some of the playwrights, critics, actors, directors and historical characters associated with Shakespeare, ranging from ancient history to the present day.

Aldridge, Ira (c. 1807-1867) Black American actor famous in Europe for his Shakespearean roles, including Othello, Macbeth and Lear. Racial prejudice at the time prevented him from performing in the United States.

Aristotle (384-322BC) Ancient Greek philosopher, scientist and author. He wrote the *Poetics*, describing the rules of Greek drama. Aristotle's work was influential in Europe in the medieval and Elizabethan periods and would have been known to Shakespeare.

Ashcroft, Peggy (1907-1991) British theatre and film actress famous for her Shakespearean roles, especially Desdemona, Juliet and Cleopatra.

Bacon, Francis (1561-1626) English writer, philosopher and politician. "Baconian" scholars think Bacon wrote Shakespeare's plays. This may be because Bacon was aristocratic and well-educated.

Branagh, Kenneth (b.1961) British actor and director. He has made and starred in films of *Henry V*, *Othello* and *Much Ado About Nothing*, *Hamlet* and *Love's Labour's Lost*, and made a film about a production of *Hamlet*, called *In the Bleak Mid-Winter*.

Brook, Peter (b.1925) Theatre and film director who has staged many Shakespeare plays. He is most famous for his innovative 1970 production of *A Midsummer Night's Dream*, featuring circus acts. He also directed a famous film version of *King Lear*.

Burbage, Richard (c.1568-1619) Leading actor in Shakespeare's theatre company, the Chamberlain's Men, and one of the greatest actors of his day. He played Hamlet, Othello and Lear, and was a friend of Shakespeare. He may also have painted Shakespeare.

Carey, Henry, Lord Hunsdon, (1524 -1596) and **George, Lord Hunsdon** (1547-1603) Henry Carey was Lord Chamberlain of England, and patron of Shakespeare's theatre company, the Chamberlain's Men, from 1594-1596. After his death his son George took his place, both as Lord Chamberlain and as patron of the Chamberlain's Men.

Coleridge, Samuel Taylor (1772-1834) Poet and critic whose works include *Shakespearean Criticism*, a collection of lectures on character and structure in Shakespeare's plays.

Dench, Judi (b.1934) British actress who has played many of Shakespeare's leading characters, such as Titania, Cleopatra, Gertrude and Lady Macbeth, in both stage and film productions.

Donne, John (c.1572-1631) Poet and, later, priest who lived at roughly the same time as Shakespeare. He is known for his love poems, which use many surprising images, and for the religious sonnets he wrote in later life.

Dryden, John (1631-1700) Poet, critic and playwright. He is now seen as the first critic to recognize Shakespeare's great importance, calling him "the father of our dramatic poets". He made studies of Shakespeare's plays and adapted *The Tempest*, *Troilus and Cressida* and *Antony and Cleopatra* (which he called *All for Love*) for the Restoration stage.

Elizabeth I (1533-1603) Daughter of Henry VIII and Anne Boleyn, and Queen of England from 1558 to 1603. Renowned for her wit, her enigmatic personality and her refusal to get married, she presided over the expansion of the theatre and the arts in late 16th-century England. She is said to have admired Shakespeare's work, and to have commissioned him to write *The Merry Wives of Windsor* because she liked the character of Falstaff in the *Henry IV* plays, and wanted a play about him.

Fletcher, John (1579-1625) Playwright who co-wrote *The Two Noble Kinsmen* and *Henry VIII* with Shakespeare. He also collaborated with Francis Beaumont, and later with another playwright called Massinger. In addition, he wrote several plays of his own.

Garrick, David (1717-1779) Actor and producer who dominated the London theatre scene in the mid-18th century. He was a student of Samuel Johnson (see opposite), began his career playing Richard III and went on to stage 24 of the plays. He did more than anyone else to popularize Shakespeare's work and made Shakespeare's home town, Stratford-upon-Avon, a tourist destination by holding a celebration there, called the "Shakespeare Jubilee", in 1769.

Gielgud, John (1904-2000) A great British actor and director. He was famous for his portrayals of Romeo, Mercutio, Malvolio, Benedick, Hamlet, Richard II, King Lear and Prospero, and appeared in many films, such as Peter Greenaway's *Prospero's Books*, which was based on *The Tempest*.

Heminge, John (1556-1630) and **Condell, Henry** (d.1627) Friends of Shakespeare who collected and edited 36 of his plays after his death, and published them in 1623 as the First Folio. At least half of them had not been published before, and the First Folio remains the earliest source of many of Shakespeare's texts. Heminge and Condell were also actors and shareholders in Shakespeare's theatre company, the Chamberlain's Men (Heminge is thought to have played Falstaff).

Henry VIII (1491-1547) King of England from 1509 to 1547, and subject of Shakespeare's late play *Henry VIII*. Famous for having six wives, he is also known for converting England from Catholicism to Protestantism. He was the father of Queen Elizabeth I. Shakespeare's play shows him in a positive light in the earlier part of his reign, though in real life he later became violent and unpredictable.

Holinshed, Raphael (c.1528-c.1580) Historian who wrote the *Chronicles of England, Scotland and Ireland*, a historical work, for Henry VII. These became the main source for many of Shakespeare's plays, including *Macbeth*, *King Lear*, *Cymbeline* and the history plays.

Hugo, François Victor (1828-1873) French writer and translator, son of the great French writer, Victor Hugo. His translation of Shakespeare's works, which was completed in 1864, is now the standard French version of Shakespeare, although there have been more recent translations.

Irving, Henry (1838-1905) Actor and producer who, along with Ellen Terry (see opposite) staged and starred in many of Shakespeare's plays in London from 1878-1902. His productions were often spectacular shows. He was even known to build real streams and use real animals such as rabbits and horses on stage, and had flying, singing witches in his version of *Macbeth*.

James I (1566-1625) James VI of Scotland became James I of England in 1603. He enjoyed the theatre, and on the death of George Carey (see opposite) he became the patron of Shakespeare's theatre company, which became the King's Men. Banquo in *Macbeth* was one of James's ancestors, and the play may have been written to impress the King.

Johnson, Samuel (1709-1784) Writer and critic, known for his witty remarks and strong opinions. He published an edition of Shakespeare's works in 1765 with an important preface and notes. He also included many Shakespearean quotations in his *Dictionary* (1755).

Jonson, Ben (1572-1637) Playwright and poet, and a friend of Shakespeare (Shakespeare acted in the early performances of some of his plays). He often had plays performed at the Globe Theatre, and is best known for his comic and satirical works. He wrote of Shakespeare that "He was not of an age, but for all time!"

Kean, Edmund (c.1789-1833) British actor, a star of the theatre in the early 19th century. His exciting, emotional style broke new ground and his Shakespeare performances - especially of Shylock, Richard III and Othello - were huge popular successes.

Kempe, Will (c.1550-c.1603) Clown in Shakespeare's theatre company, the Chamberlain's Men. He left the company in 1599. In 1600 he performed his "Nine daies wonder" - a folk dance along the road from London to Norwich.

Kurosawa, Akira (b.1910) Japanese film director famous for his film adaptations of *Macbeth* (*Throne of Blood*, 1957) and *King Lear* (*Ran*, 1985). Both are set in medieval Japan and are heavily adapted. They are very exciting to watch.

Lamb, Charles (1775-1834) and **Mary** (1764-1847) Charles Lamb, a critic and writer, and his sister Mary retold the stories of 20 of Shakespeare's plays in a book for children called *Tales from Shakespeare* (1807). They removed some of the ruder and more complicated parts of the plays.

Lennox, Charlotte (1720-1804) English writer who analyzed the sources of more than half of Shakespeare's plays, and published a collection of them called *Shakespear Illustrated; or the Novels and Histories on which the plays are founded*, in 1753.

Malone, Edmond (1741-1812) Great Shakespeare scholar who published a huge ten-volume edition of Shakespeare's works, with a long account of Shakespeare's life, in 1790. He also studied the history of the theatre during Shakespeare's lifetime, researching diaries, account books and other material from the period, and attempted to find out the order in which Shakespeare wrote his plays. Malone's work is the basis of much modern scholarship on Shakespeare.

Marlowe, Christopher (1564-1593) Playwright born in the same year as Shakespeare, and renowned as a great writer by the time of his death aged 29, when he was killed, apparently in a tavern fight. Like Shakespeare, he was a tradesman's son, but unlike him, he went to a university. He planned to become a priest, but in fact may have been a government spy, and was later accused of atheism. Marlowe's plays include *Tamburlaine* (1587), *Edward II* (1592) and *Dr. Faustus* (1592).

Middleton, Thomas (c. 1570-1627) Playwright who may have worked with Shakespeare on *Timon of Athens* and possibly *Macbeth*, although experts do not all agree about this. Middleton's own plays include *Women Beware Women* (c.1621), *The Changeling* (c. 1622) and *A Game At Chess* (1624).

Olivier, Laurence (1907-1989) A great British actor and director of the 20th century. Among other work, he played most of Shakespeare's leading roles on the stage, directed and starred in films of *Henry V*, *Hamlet* and *Richard III*, and starred in films of *Othello* and *King Lear*.

Poel, William (1852-1934) English theatre producer. He reacted against the spectacular style of 19th-century Shakespearean productions, such as those by Irving (see opposite) and Tree (see right). In 1894 he formed the Elizabethan Stage Society, which aimed to recreate the original effect of Elizabethan performances, using a minimum of scenery.

Rowe, Nicholas (1674-1718) A playwright who published important new editions of Shakespeare's works in 1709 and 1714. He added extra stage directions and "dramatis personae" (lists of characters) to the plays, and divided them into acts and scenes. He also wrote a biography of Shakespeare as a preface to his editions.

Schlegel, August Wilhelm von (1767-1845) German poet who, working with his wife Karoline Schelling, translated many of Shakespeare's plays into German. The translations were completed later by Ludwig Tieck, and the "Schlegel-Tieck Shakespeare" is still the standard version of Shakespeare in German.

Siddons, Sarah (1755-1831) Leading English actress in the late 18th and early 19th centuries. She specialized in tragic and heroic roles, and was famous for her Shakespearean roles, especially Lady Macbeth.

Terry, Ellen (1848-1928) Leading British actress of the late 19th and early 20th centuries She worked mostly with the theatre company of Henry Irving (see opposite) and often starred opposite him, playing most of Shakespeare's female lead roles.

Tree, Herbert Beerbohm (1853-1917) Actor and producer who, as manager of the Haymarket Theatre in London, staged and starred in many elaborate Shakespeare productions. He was the last producer to use the lavish style popular in the 19th century.

Wanamaker, Sam (1919-1993) American actor who started the project to rebuild Shakespeare's Globe Theatre in London, near its original site by the River Thames. Building work on the theatre began in 1987, but Wanamaker died in 1993, before it was completed.

Webster, John (c.1578-c.1623) English Jacobean playwright. His two plays *The White Devil* (1612) and *The Duchess of Malfi* (1614), are powerful examples of revenge tragedy, and have been popular in the 20th century.

Welles, Orson (1915-1985) American actor and director who directed and starred in films of *Macbeth* (1946) and *Othello* (1952), and made a film version of both parts of *Henry IV* called *Chimes at Midnight* (1965).

Wriothesley, Henry, Earl of Southampton (1573-1624) Aristocrat, to whom Shakespeare dedicated the two poems *Venus and Adonis* (1593) and *The Rape of Lucrece* (1594). Scholars have also suggested that he may be the young man addressed in Shakespeare's sonnets.

Zeffirelli, Franco (b.1923) Italian stage and film director. He filmed *The Taming of the Shrew* in 1966, *Romeo and Juliet* in 1968, and *Hamlet*, starring Mel Gibson, in 1990.

Glossary of terms and phrases

act A section of a play. Shakespeare's plays are always divided into five acts, though he himself didn't divide them in this way.

anti-Semitism Racial prejudice against, or hatred of, Jewish people.

apron stage A stage that extends out into the audience.

avant-garde Experimental or daringly modern.

bad quarto A quarto (see right) with an unreliable text, sometimes based on an actor's memory of a play.

catharsis A word used by Aristotle to describe the release of emotions such as fear and pity through seeing them enacted in a dramatic tragedy.

Catholic, Roman Of or belonging to the Christian Church of Rome, founded in the 4th century AD.

Chain of Being The concept that everything in the universe is ranked in a strict order, with God at the top.

Civil War The war of 1642-48 in England between the Royalists, loyal to Charles I, and the Parliamentarians, led by the Puritan Oliver Cromwell.

clown In Shakespeare's time, an actor specializing in comic roles.

comedy A play with a happy ending.

critic Someone who studies and analyzes literature or other kinds of art.

director The person who controls the artistic aspects of a production.

Elizabethan Of or related to the reign of Elizabeth I (1558-1603).

excommunicate To expel someone from the Roman Catholic Church.

exile Banishment to another country.

fair copy A copy of the script of a play, written out neatly for actors to use in rehearsals.

farce A comic play or scene involving physical or ridiculous comedy.

fatal flaw Used by Aristotle to mean a character trait which contributes to the downfall of a character in tragedy. It has been used by some critics to describe Shakespeare's tragedies, but other critics argue that Shakespeare did not adhere to Aristotle's ideas about drama.

feminism A movement advocating equal rights for women.

figure of speech A way of using language in an unusual sense, such as a simile or a metaphor (see right), in order to describe something vividly.

First Folio The first collected edition of Shakespeare's works, published in 1623.

fool A kind of jester (see right).

foot or **metrical foot** A unit of poetic rhythm, usually made up of two or three syllables.

foul papers The original handwritten manuscripts of a play.

good quarto A quarto (see right) based on an original manuscript.

hamartia The Greek name for the fatal flaw (see left).

history play A play that retells a historical story, usually about royalty.

humours The four fluids: black bile, phlegm, blood and choler, which were thought to exist in the human body and affect personality.

iambic foot or **iamb** A foot (see above) made up of an unstressed syllable followed by a stressed one.

iambic pentameter A line of verse made up of five iambic feet (see above).

imagery the use of images, such as metaphors and similes (see right), for descriptive or symbolic effect.

Jacobean Of or related to the reign of James I (1603-1625).

jester A servant paid to entertain or amuse his employer.

jig A comic song and dance routine which, in Shakespeare's time, was usually performed after a play.

literary criticism The academic study and evaluation of literatire.

masque A type of formal dramatic entertainment, often with music, dance and songs.

medieval Of or relating to the Middle Ages (see below).

metaphor A figure of speech (see left) in which something is described in a way that is not literally true, such as "All the world's a stage" (*As You Like It*).

Middle Ages Period in European history dating from c.1000 to c.1500.

morality play A type of medieval play in which characters represented moral qualities, such as sins and virtues.

mystery play A medieval play which retold biblical stories.

oracle In ancient Greek folklore, a religious shrine, or a god-given message revealed there.

pagan A name for any pre-Christian religion, often with many gods, or a follower of such a religion.

pastoral Literature that has an idealized countryside theme.

pathos A quality in literature that arouses feelings of pity or sorrow.

patron Someone who supports a writer or other artist financially.

plague An epidemic disease, spread by rat fleas.

plot The story told by a literary work.

problem play Name given to a type of play that seems morally unresolved and has no clear conclusion.

prophecy A prediction from a mystical source, such as a witch.

props Objects used on stage during a performance of a play.

protagonist The hero or main character of a play, especially a tragedy.

Protestant Of or belonging to a non-Catholic (see left) Christian Church, founded after Martin Luther rebelled against the Church of Rome in 1529.

Puritan An extreme Protestant (see above). Puritans believed in self-denial and were often opposed to public entertainment such as theatre.

quarto An early, printed edition of a single Shakespeare play.

Reformation The break from the Roman Catholic (see left) Church which led to the founding of Protestant (see above) churches.

Renaissance The name given to major developments in art and culture in Europe, from approximately the 14th to the 17th centuries.

Restoration The return of the monarchy in 1660, after the English Civil War (see left) and the rule of Cromwell.

rhetoric The art of persuasive or emotive speaking.

rhyme scheme The rhyme pattern in a particular poem or type of poem.

rhyming couplet Two rhyming lines of verse next to each other.

romance A name for a play with tragic and comic elements and themes of forgiveness and reconciliation.

satire Literature which attacks ideas or people by ridiculing them.

scene A small section of a play. Acts (see left) are usually divided into scenes.

scholarship Academic study.

set The scenery for a production.

simile A figure of speech (see left) in which one thing is compared to another, such as "mine own tears /Do scald like molten lead" (*King Lear*).

sonnet A fourteen-line poem with a strict rhyme scheme (see above).

subplot A secondary plot in a play.

tragedy A play in which the hero cannot cope with his situation, usually ending in his death and that of others.

tragicomedy A play in which tragic events have a happy outcome.

Wars of the Roses The English civil wars of 1455-1480 between the houses of Lancaster and York.

Glossary of Shakespearean words

Shakespeare used hundreds of words which are unfamiliar to modern readers. This glossary explains some of these words. In a play, you can often guess what a word means from the context (the other words around it).

a sometimes used to mean "he"
abate to reduce or subdue
abuse to deceive
affection passions or feelings
affright to frighten, to make tremble
aim a guess or a suspicion
alarum a call to battle
allay to relieve or reassure
anon soon, presently
arras a curtain or wall-hanging
art are ("thou art" means "you are")
art artifice, cunning
aspect a look or glance
balm soothing oil or ointment
barn or **bairn** a child
bastard sweet Spanish wine
beard refers to someone's manhood
beldam a grandmother or old hag
betwixt between
blunt stupid or unsophisticated
bodkin a dagger or pin
bosom heart, or heartfelt feelings
bound tied up or imprisoned
brabble to fight or quarrel
caitiff a wretch or miserable person
care a worry or concern
casques cannons
chair sometimes means the throne
chaps jaws or mouth
ciphers actors, people in disguise
clerk a scholar or academic
cock-pit a theatre
company a companion
complexion a mood or state of affairs
con to know, learn or study
conceit an idea or opinion
cony a rabbit
couch to lie down or hide
countenance false show, hypocrisy
craft craftiness or cunning
crown a king (also a type of coin)
cuckold a man whose wife is being unfaithful
cunning knowledge, skill, cleverness
date a period of time
defend to forbid
discharge to do one's duty, or to dismiss someone
disease uneasiness or trouble
dispatch to kill, to send away, or to hurry
dissemble to deceive or pretend
doff or **daff** to take off (e.g. a hat)

dole allowance or sadness
doubt to suspect or fear
ducats European coins
ecstasy excitement or madness
ere before
excrements beard, hair, fingernails
eyne eyes
face appearance, especially if false
fathom six feet in depth
fell cruel, fierce
fie! an expression of anger or shock
fig to insult
foison riches, plenty
folly foolishness, madness
fond foolish, weak, or doting
fordo to kill
foul ugly, dirty, muddy, or evil
frenzy agitation or a fever
froward rebellious, stubborn
fulsome filthy, disgusting
gaberdine a cloak
gallows a structure for public hangings
gentle noble, civilized
gib a tomcat
go to! an expression of disbelief
government self-control
gouts drops (of blood)
gramercy thank you (short for "God have mercy")
green young and inexperienced
gull to trick or cheat someone
hail greetings, welcome
happy fortunate, lucky
hast have ("thou hast" means "you have")
hath have ("he hath" means "he has")
heavy slow, sad, or stupid
hedge-pig a hedgehog
hereafter later, the future
hit to agree or succeed
hold to value someone or something
humorous changeable in mood
hurly noise
ill bad, evil, or with bad intentions
incarnadine to stain red
insensible impossible to perceive
intelligence news, information
issue children or descendants
keel to skim
kindless unnatural
kindly naturally
lease a period of time
leman sweetheart or lover
let to stop or prevent
lustihood vitality or strength
marry! indeed, certainly
match an agreement, appointment or pairing
mate to dismay or confound, also means to marry
meat any kind of food
metal strength

mirth comedy, jokes
misery greed
modern everyday, trivial
much strange, wonderful, very
nephew grandson, any male relative
nice delicate, precise, fussy
owe to own
pash to hit violently
pedant schoolteacher
perchance perhaps
perdee indeed
pied patterned with two shades
plenty wealth, abundance
points small tags or ties on clothing
pregnant full of meaning, obvious
pretty little, insignificant
prithee please (short for "I pray thee")
quat a spot, zit or pimple
quell to murder, kill or destroy
quick alive, lively
rail to scream, shout, scold or abuse
rate to tell off, or to evaluate
rear-mouse a bat
reck to care or mind
sack white wine
sad serious
saucy provocative, lascivious, sexual
scarce hardly
seamy greasy
shrew a nagging, angry woman
silly innocent, simple
simple foolish
sirrah sir
skill cunning, cleverness
slobbery sloppy
slubber to make dirty, or to hurry
sooth truth or sweetness
soothsayer fortune-teller
sport games, fun
steal to creep, sneak up
sway power, influence
tarry to wait, delay, hang around
temperate moderate, calm
thee you (used to children, friends, lovers or inferiors such as servants)
thou you (used when being polite)
thy (familiar) or **thine** (polite) your
tickle-brain strong alcoholic drink
tidings news
'tis it is
'twas it was
unrough smooth-chinned, i.e. young
use a habit or custom; also means to lend money
vasty big, vast
watch a night watchman
welkin the sky
wench a young woman
wit sense, sanity
worm a snake
ye you
zany a fool

Glossary of Shakespearean characters

This is a guide to some of the main characters in Shakespeare's plays. Some names of plays are abbreviated.

Key to abbreviations

1 Henry IV	Henry IV Part 1
2 Henry IV	Henry IV Part 2
1 Henry VI	Henry VI Part 1
2 Henry VI	Henry VI Part 2
3 Henry VI	Henry VI Part 3
2GV	Two Gentlemen of Verona
2NK	The Two Noble Kinsmen
12th Night	Twelfth Night
A&C	Antony and Cleopatra
All's Well	All's Well That Ends Well
AYLI	As You Like It
Errors	The Comedy of Errors
JC	Julius Caesar
K John	King John
K Lear	King Lear
LLL	Love's Labour's Lost
M for M	Measure for Measure
Merchant	The Merchant of Venice
MND	A Midsummer Night's Dream
Much Ado	Much Ado About Nothing
R&J	Romeo and Juliet
Shrew	The Taming of the Shrew
T&C	Troilus and Cressida
Timon	Timon of Athens
Titus	Titus Andronicus
W Tale	The Winter's Tale
Wives	The Merry Wives of Windsor

Aaron Tamora's lover in *Titus*.
Achilles Greek warrior in *T&C*.
Aguecheek, Sir Andrew Comic, foolish knight in *12th Night*.
Albany, Duke of Good husband of Goneril, Lear's daughter, in *K Lear*.
Aliena The name used by Celia in *AYLI* when she escapes to the forest.
Alonso King of Naples in *The Tempest*.
Angelo Corrupt deputy who stands in for the Duke in *M for M*.
Anne The Pages' daughter in *Wives*.
Antigonus Lord in *W Tale*.
Antipholus of Ephesus and **Antipholus of Syracuse** Twins in *Errors*.
Antonio The merchant in *Merchant*.
Antonio Prospero's usurping brother in *The Tempest*.
Antonio Sea captain in *12th Night*.
Antony, Mark Roman soldier and politician who appears in *JC* and *A&C*.
Arcite One of the kinsmen in *2NK*.
Ariel Magic spirit in *The Tempest*.
Armado, Don Visiting Spanish gentleman in *LLL*.
Arthur The King's nephew who has a claim to the throne in *K John*.

Arviragus One of the King's long-lost sons in *Cymbeline*.
Aufidius Volscian general, enemy of the Romans in *Coriolanus*.
Autolycus Clown in *W Tale*.
Balthasar The name used by Portia in *Merchant* when disguised as a lawyer.
Banquo Macbeth's friend in *Macbeth*.
Baptista Katherine's father in *Shrew*.
Bardolph Friend of Falstaff in *1* and *2 Henry IV* and *Henry V*.
Bassanio Antonio's friend in *Merchant*.
Beatrice Witty heroine of *Much Ado*.
Belarius Banished lord in *Cymbeline*.
Belch, Sir Toby Olivia's uncle in *12th Night*.
Benedick A bachelor who secretly loves Beatrice in *Much Ado*.
Berowne or **Birun** Courtier in *LLL*.
Bertram Helena's unwilling husband in *All's Well*.
Bianca Katherine's sister in *Shrew*.
Bolingbroke, Henry Cousin of the King in *Richard II*, becomes Henry IV.
Bottom Weaver and leader of the troupe of amateur actors in *MND*.
Brabantio Desdemona's father in *Othello*.
Brutus Conspirator in *JC*.
Buckingham, Duke of Nobleman executed for treason in *Henry VIII*.
Buckingham, Duke of An ally, then an enemy, of Richard in *Richard III*.
Bullen, Anne (Anne Boleyn) Henry's second wife in *Henry VIII*.
Cade, Jack Rebel in *2 Henry VI*.
Caesar, Julius Roman leader in *JC*.
Caesar, Octavius Roman politician in *JC* and *A&C*.
Caliban Savage slave in *The Tempest*.
Calpurnia Caesar's wife in *JC*.
Casca Conspirator in *JC*.
Cassio Soldier in *Othello*.
Cassius Conspirator in *JC*.
Celia Rosalind's cousin in *AYLI*.
Cesario Name Viola takes when disguised as a boy in *12th Night*.
Clarence, George, Duke of Brother of Edward IV and Richard III. Appears in *3 Henry VI* and *Richard III*.
Claudio Young gentleman in *M for M*.
Claudio Young soldier in *Much Ado*.
Claudius Danish king in *Hamlet*.
Cleon Governor of Tarsus in *Pericles*.
Cleopatra Queen of Egypt in *A&C*.
Cloten Queen's son in *Cymbeline*.
Cordelia Lear's youngest daughter in *K Lear*.
Corin Old shepherd in *AYLI*.
Coriolanus Roman hero in *Coriolanus*.
Cornwall, Duke of Evil husband of Regan, Lear's daughter, in *K Lear*.

Cressida Troilus's lover in *T&C*.
Cymbeline King of Britian in *Cymbeline*.
Demetrius Young lover in *MND*.
Desdemona Othello's wife in *Othello*.
Diana Young woman in *All's Well*.
Diomedes Cressida's lover in *T&C*.
Dionyza Cleon's wife in *Pericles*.
Dogberry Constable in *Much Ado*.
Dromio of Ephesus and **Dromio of Syracuse** Twin slaves in *Errors*.
Duke Frederick *see* Frederick, Duke.
Duke of Milan Duke in *2GV*.
Duke Senior *see* Senior, Duke.
Duke of Vienna Duke in *M for M*.
Dumaine Courtier in *LLL*.
Duncan Scottish king in *Macbeth*.
Edgar Gloucester's son in *K Lear*.
Edmund Gloucester's bastard son in *K Lear*.
Edward IV Richard Plantagenet's son in *3 Henry VI*, and king in *Richard III*.
Egeon Old man of Syracuse in *Errors*.
Elizabeth Widow of Edward IV in *Richard III*, and an enemy of Richard.
Emilia Egeon's lost wife in *Errors*.
Emilia Lady-in-waiting in *Othello*.
Emilia Theseus's sister-in-law in *2NK*.
Enobarbus Soldier and Antony's best friend in *A&C*.
Escalus Old judge in *M for M*.
Falstaff, Sir John Drunken knight in *1* and *2 Henry IV*, *Henry V* and *Wives*.
Fenton Young man in *Wives*.
Ferdinand Son of Alonso, and Miranda's suitor, in *The Tempest*.
Feste Clown in *12th Night*.
Fidele Name Imogen takes when disguised as a boy in *Cymbeline*.
Fleance Banquo's son in *Macbeth*.
Florizel Polixenes's son in *W Tale*.
Fool Lear's jester in *K Lear*.
Ford Wealthy husband in *Wives*.
Ford, Mistress Lady in *Wives*.
Frederick, Duke Usurping brother of Duke Senior in *AYLI*.
Friar Laurence *see* Laurence, Friar.
Ganymede Name Rosalind takes when disguised as a boy in *AYLI*.
Gaunt, John of In *Richard II*, father of Bolingbroke and adviser to Richard.
Gertrude Queen in *Hamlet*.
Gloucester, Duke of King's uncle in *1* and *2 Henry VI*. Also appears in *Henry IV* as Prince Hal's brother.
Gloucester, Earl of Earl in *K Lear*.
Goneril Lear's daughter in *K Lear*.
Gonzalo Statesman in *The Tempest*.
Gratiano Bassanio's friend in *Merchant*.
Guidarius One of the King's long-lost sons in *Cymbeline*.
Guildenstern Courtier in *Hamlet*.

Hal Nickname of Prince Harry, the King's son in *1* and *2 Henry IV*. He becomes King Henry V.

Hamlet Prince of Denmark in *Hamlet*.

Hector Trojan prince in *T&C*.

Helena Heroine of *All's Well*.

Helena Young lover in *MND*.

Henry, Prince King's son in *K John*.

Hermia Young lover in *MND*.

Hermione Queen in *W Tale*.

Hero Beautiful heroine in *Much Ado*.

Hippolyta Duchess in *MND & 2NK*.

Holofernes Schoolmaster in *LLL*.

Horatio Hamlet's friend in *Hamlet*.

Hotspur Nickname of Henry Percy, who rebels against the King in *1 Henry IV*.

Iachimo A villain in *Cymbeline*.

Iago Scheming soldier in *Othello*.

Imogen King's daughter in *Cymbeline*.

Isabella Claudio's sister in *M for M*.

Jaques Melancholy lord in *AYLI*.

Jessica Shylock's daughter in *Merchant*.

Joan La Pucelle Joan of Arc, a French warrior in *1 Henry VI*.

John, Don Don Pedro's evil brother in *Much Ado*.

Julia Heroine of *2GV*.

Juliet Claudio's fiancée in *M for M*.

Juliet Romantic heroine of *R&J*.

Julius Caesar *see* Caesar, Julius.

Katherine Princess of France who marries Henry in *Henry V*.

Katherine Queen in *Henry VIII*.

Katherine Bad-tempered, argumentative heroine of *Shrew*.

Kent, Earl of Nobleman in *K Lear*.

King of France King in *All's Well*.

King of France Cordelia's husband in *K Lear*.

King of Navarre King in *LLL*.

Lady Macbeth *See* Macbeth, Lady.

Laertes Ophelia's brother in *Hamlet*.

Laurence, Friar Friar in *R&J*.

Lavinia Titus's daughter in *Titus*.

Lear, King British king in *K Lear*.

Leonato Governor of Messina in *Much Ado*.

Leontes King of Sicily in *W Tale*.

Lepidus Roman politician who appears in *JC* and *A&C*.

Longaville Courtier in *LLL*.

Lucius Roman general in *Cymbeline*.

Lysander Young lover in *MND*.

Macbeth Scottish thane (lord), and later King of Scotland, in *Macbeth*.

Macbeth, Lady Macbeth's ambitious, unscrupulous wife in *Macbeth*.

Macduff Soldier in *Macbeth*.

Malcolm Duncan's son in *Macbeth*.

Malvolio Steward in *12th Night*.

Mamillius Leontes's son in *W Tale*.

Margaret Queen in *1, 2* and *3 Henry VI*. Also appears in *Richard III*.

Mariana Angelo's abandoned fiancée in *M for M*.

Mark Antony see Antony, Mark.

Mercutio Romeo's friend in *R&J*.

Milan, Duke of *see* Duke of Milan.

Miranda Prospero's daughter in *The Tempest*.

Mowbray, Thomas Duke of Norfolk banished by the King in *Richard II*.

Nerissa Portia's maid in *Merchant*.

Northumberland, Earl of Hotspur's father in *1* and *2 Henry IV*.

Nurse Juliet's servant in *R&J*.

Nym Friend of Falstaff in *Henry V* and *Wives*.

Oberon King of the fairies in *MND*.

Octavius Caesar see Caesar, Octavius.

Oliver Orlando's brother in *AYLI*.

Olivia Wealthy lady in *12th Night*.

Ophelia Daughter of Polonius in *Hamlet*.

Orlando Brave hero of *AYLI*.

Orsino Duke in *12th Night*.

Othello Venetian general in *Othello*.

Overdone, Mistress Brothel-keeper in *M for M*.

Page Wealthy husband in *Wives*.

Page, Mistress Lady in *Wives*.

Palamon One of the kinsmen in *2NK*.

Paris Suitor for Juliet in *R&J*.

Parolles Bertram's friend in *All's Well*.

Paulina Lady in *W Tale*.

Pedro, Don Prince of Aragon in *Much Ado*.

Perdita Leontes's daughter in *W Tale*.

Petruchio Katherine's suitor, and then husband, in *Shrew*.

Phoebe Shepherdess in *AYLI*.

Pistol Friend of Falstaff in *2 Henry IV*, *Henry V* and *Wives*.

Poins Friend of Falstaff in *1* and *2 Henry IV*.

Polixenes King of Bohemia and friend of Leontes in *W Tale*.

Polonius Old lord in *Hamlet*.

Pompey Roman rebel in *A&C*.

Pompey Petty criminal in *M for M*.

Poor Tom Name Edgar takes when disguised in *K Lear*.

Portia Wife of Brutus in *JC*.

Portia Beautiful, wealthy and wise heiress in *Merchant*.

Posthumus Imogen's husband in *Cymbeline*.

Princess of France Daughter of the King of France in *LLL*.

Prospero Exiled Duke of Milan in *The Tempest*.

Proteus Young gentleman in *2GV*.

Puck Mischievous fairy in *MND*.

Queen Wife of the King and stepmother to Imogen in *Cymbeline*.

Quickly, Mistress Servant in *Wives* and hostess of a tavern in *1* and *2 Henry IV* and *Henry V*.

Regan Lear's daughter in *K Lear*.

Richmond, Henry Tudor, Earl of Nobleman who defeats Richard in *Richard III*. Also appears in *3 Henry VI*. Was later to become Henry VII.

Romeo Young lover, hero of *R&J*.

Rosalind Bold heroine of *AYLI*.

Rosencrantz Courtier in *Hamlet*.

Roussillon, Countess of Bertram's mother in *All's Well*.

Sebastian Alonso's evil brother in *The Tempest*.

Sebastian Viola's brother in *12th Night*.

Senior, Duke Rightful duke in *AYLI*.

Shylock Money-lender in *Merchant*.

Silvia Duke's daughter in *2GV*.

Silvius Young shepherd in *AYLI*.

Somerset, Duke of Duke on the Lancastrian side in *1* and *2 Henry VI*.

Stephano Butler in *The Tempest*.

Suffolk, Earl of Earl in *1 Henry VI*.

Suffolk, William de la Pole, Duke of Nobleman in *1* and *2 Henry VI*.

Talbot English war hero against the French in *1 Henry VI*.

Tamora Queen of the Goths in *Titus*.

Theseus Duke of Athens in *MND*, and also in *2NK*.

Timon Bankrupt Athenian in *Timon*.

Titania Fairy queen in *MND*.

Titus Andronicus Roman general in *Titus*.

Touchstone Clown in *AYLI*.

Trinculo Jester in *The Tempest*.

Troilus Trojan prince, hero of *T&C*.

Tybalt Enemy of Romeo in *R&J*.

Valentine Young gentleman in *2GV*.

Verges Constable in *Much Ado*.

Vienna, Duke of *see* Duke of Vienna.

Viola Heroine of *12th Night*.

Virgilia Coriolanus's wife in *Coriolanus*.

Volumnia Coriolanus's mother in *Coriolanus*.

Witches Three women who foretell Macbeth's fate in *Macbeth*.

Wolsey, Cardinal Powerful Catholic cardinal in *Henry VIII*.

York, Richard Plantagenet, Duke of Would-be king in *1, 2* and *3 Henry VI*. He dies in *Part 3*.

York, Scrope, Archbishop of Archbishop who opposes the King in in *2 Henry IV*.

Important dates

1558 Elizabeth, daugher of Henry VIII and Anne Boleyn, becomes Queen of England.

1564 Dramatist Christopher Marlowe is born.

23 April: On or around this date, William Shakespeare is born in Henley St., Stratford-upon-Avon, the third child of John Shakespeare and Mary Arden. This is Shakespeare's official birthday: his exact date of birth is uncertain.

26 April: Shakespeare is baptized in Stratford.

1567 Actor Richard Burbage is born.

1568 John Shakespeare is elected bailiff of Stratford.

1569 Elizabeth I crushes the Northern Rising, a Catholic rebellion in the north of England.

1570 Pope Pius V excommunicates Elizabeth I.

1572 Dramatist Ben Jonson is born.

1576 John Shakespeare is near bankruptcy.
The Theatre opens in Shoreditch, north of the City of London.

1577 The Curtain Theatre opens in London.

1582 **28 November:** William Shakespeare marries Anne Hathaway.

1583 **26 May:** Baptism of Susanna, first child of William and Anne.

1585 **2 February:** Baptism of Hamnet and Judith, twins of William and Anne.

1587 Mary Queen of Scots is executed. The theatre companies the Queen's Men and Leicester's Men perform in Stratford. Shakespeare is thought to have left Stratford for London at around this time, possibly with one of the acting companies.
The Rose Theatre opens on Bankside in London.

1588 The Spanish Armada (fleet) is destroyed off the coast of southern England.

1589 At about this time, Shakespeare starts work on his first plays – the historical trilogy of *Henry VI*.

1592– London's theatres are closed because of an outbreak
1594 of plague.

1593 Christopher Marlowe dies at Deptford in London.

1595 The Swan Theatre built at Bankside in London.

1596 **11 August:** Shakespeare's son Hamnet dies aged 11.

1597 Shakespeare buys New Place, a large house in Stratford-upon-Avon, for £60.
Shakespeare acts in Ben Jonson's comedy *Every Man in His Humour*.

1598– The Theatre is dismantled, rebuilt on the south
1599 bank of the River Thames in London, and renamed The Globe. Shakespeare and other members of his theatre company, the Chamberlain's Men, hold shares in it.

1601 Shakespeare's father, John Shakespeare, dies.

1603 Elizabeth I dies. James VI of Scotland becomes James I of England. The Chamberlain's Men become the King's Men.

1603– 30,000 die of the plague in London. The theatres
1604 are closed again.

1605 **5 November:** Guy Fawkes and others try to blow up the Houses of Parliament in London, in the "Gunpowder Plot".

1607 **5 June:** Susanna, Shakespeare's elder daughter, marries John Hall, a doctor in Stratford.

1608 The King's Men take over Blackfriars Theatre.

1610 Shakespeare returns to live at New Place.

1613 **29 June:** The Globe burns down.

1614 **30 June:** The rebuilt Globe reopens.

1616 **10 February:** Shakespeare's younger daughter Judith marries Thomas Quiney.

25 March: Shakespeare signs his will.

23 April (probably his 52nd birthday): William Shakespeare dies.

25 April: Shakespeare is buried in Stratford at Holy Trinity Church.

1623 Anne Shakespeare dies.
The First Folio is published.

Dates of Shakespeare's works

We cannot be sure about when Shakespeare wrote his works, but experts have made guesses based on historical references and the original dates when the works were printed. The dates shown here are mostly estimates, but they give an idea of the general order of Shakespeare's works.

Plays

1589-92	*Henry VI Part 1, Henry VI Part 2, Henry VI Part 3*
1592-3	*Richard III, Titus Andronicus*
1593-4	*The Comedy of Errors, The Taming of the Shrew*
1594-5	*The Two Gentlemen of Verona, Love's Labour's Lost*
1595-6	*Romeo and Juliet, Richard II, A Midsummer Night's Dream*
1596-7	*King John, The Merchant of Venice*
1597-8	*Henry IV Part 1, Henry IV Part 2*
1598-9	*Much Ado About Nothing, Henry V, The Merry Wives of Windsor*
1599-1600	*Julius Caesar, As You Like It*
1600-1	*Hamlet, Twelfth Night*
1601-2	*Troilus and Cressida*
1602-3	*All's Well That Ends Well, Othello*
1603-4	*Measure for Measure*
1604-5	*King Lear*
1605-6	*Macbeth*
1606-7	*Antony and Cleopatra, Timon of Athens*
1607-8	*Coriolanus, Pericles*
1609-10	*Cymbeline*
1610-11	*The Winter's Tale*
1611-12	*The Tempest*
1612-13	*Henry VIII* (co-written with John Fletcher)
1613-14	*The Two Noble Kinsmen* (co-written with John Fletcher)

Poems

1593	*Venus and Adonis*
1594	*The Rape of Lucrece*
1609	*The Sonnets*

Lost Works

Pre-1598	*Love's Labour's Won*
Pre-1613	*Cardenio* (co-written with John Fletcher)

Shakespeare Web sites

If you have access to the Internet, you can find out more about Shakespeare's life and works by visiting the Web sites listed here. For direct links to all the sites, go to **www.usborne-quicklinks.com** and enter the keyword **shakespeare**. Enter this page number, and you will see a list of the Web sites described below. Click on the number of the site you want to visit.

General sites

Web site 1 A huge and well-organized collection of links to Web sites on every Shakespearean theme imaginable, from detailed studies of the plays to references in Star Trek.

Web site 2 Another well-designed site that's easy to navigate and use, with lots of information and useful links to other sites on Shakespeare's life and times, the plays, language and Elizabethan theatre.

Web site 3 A site maintained by the University of Victoria in Canada. Some articles and discussions are quite advanced, but there is an excellent section on Shakespeare's life and times, as well as studies of the plays, in the **Library** area of the site.

Web site 4 If you have a question about anything at all to do with Shakespeare, check this site. Your question may have been answered already, otherwise you can send it in to a panel of Shakespeare experts.

Web site 5 The complete works of Shakespeare available online.

Web site 6 A specialist Shakespeare search, this allows you to find a quotation from the plays starting from only a few words. There's also a poetry search on **Web site 7**.

Web site 8 If you are studying Shakespeare, you will find lots of useful articles on this site, produced by an English teacher.

Web site 9 If you're finding Shakespeare a drag, this site aims to help, with bright graphics, quizzes and games as well as study guides.

The "authorship problem"

Web site 10 Did Shakespeare actually write the plays? Here's a good summary of the long-running debate.

Shakespeare on film

Web site 11 Here you can find details of every film ever based on Shakespeare's works, from the present day back to 1899.

Some recent film versions have very stylish Web sites, which may include stills from the film, directors' notes, study guides and e-cards to send to your friends. At **www.usborne-quicklinks.com** you'll find links to the following:

Titus (**Web site 12**), directed by Julie Taymor (1999). A powerful vision of this bloodthirsty tragedy.

A Midsummer Night's Dream (**Web site 13**), directed by Michael Hoffmann (1999). A traditionally romantic production.

William Shakespeare's Romeo + Juliet (**Web site 14**), directed by Baz Luhrmann (1996). A spectacular contemporary *Romeo and Juliet*.

Twelfth Night (**Web site 15**), directed by Trevor Nunn (1996). An Edwardian house-party atmosphere.

Hamlet (**Web site 16**), directed by Kenneth Branagh (1996). An actor-director's insights.

Shakespeare on stage

In the UK:
Web site 17 A complete list of current productions in the UK, and when and where you can see them.

Web site 18 The home page of the UK's best-known Shakespeare company, the Royal Shakespeare Company.

Web site 19 You can see Shakespeare plays in the open air at this summer festival in Cambridge.

Festivals in the US:
There are over a hundred Shakespeare festivals in different states across the US, and many have Web sites giving details of future productions. Some are listed below, and you can find many others through the **Shakespeare Festivals and Companies** page on **Web site 20**.

The Public Theater (**Web site 21**) (Central Park, New York)

Cleveland Shakespeare Festival (**Web site 22**) (Ohio)

The Shakespeare Theatre (**Web site 23**) (Washington, D.C.)

Alabama Shakespeare Festival (**Web site 24**)

Dallas Shakespeare Festival (**Web site 25**) (Texas)

Utah Shakespeare Festival (**Web site 26**)

Oregon Shakespeare Festival (**Web site 27**)

Shakespeare By The Sea (**Web site 28**) (Los Angeles, California)

In Canada:
Bard on the Beach (**Web site 29**) (Vancouver, B.C.)

Stratford Festival (**Web site 30**) (Stratford, Ontario)

In Australia:
Bell Shakespeare Company (**Web site 31**)

Just for fun

Web site 32 Roll the dice for a random selection of typical words from Shakespeare, then try to arrange them as phrases.

Web site 33 *Timon* isn't normally considered a comedy – but have you seen the dachshund version?

Web site 34 Test your knowledge, or have a guess: fill in the last word in a rhyming couplet.

Web site 35 Generate your own Shakespearean-style insults.

Index

Page numbers in italics indicate illustrations.

acting styles, 18, 38, 39, 40-41
actor-managers, 38
actors, 11, 14, 40, 41, 42, 43, 44, 45
actresses, 11, 38, 39
acts, 3, 56
Alchemist, The, 14
Aldridge, Ira, 54
Alleyn, Edward, 14
alliteration, 34
All's Well That Ends Well, 22, 24, *24,* 48, 60
anti-Semitism, 37, 40, 56
Antony and Cleopatra, 16, 20, *20,* 21, 34, *34,* 36, 39, 48, 54, 60
apron stage, 12, 56
Arden, Mary, 4, 60
Aristotle, 54, 56
art, 46
As You Like It, 22, 23, *23,* 36, *36,* 48, 60
Ashcroft, Peggy, 39, 54
assonance, 34
astrology, 7, *7,* 17
Astrophel and Stella, 32
audiences, 11, 12
auditions, 42, 43
avant-garde productions, 39, 56

Bacon, Francis, 3, 54
bad quartos, 56
Bernstein, Leonard, 47
Birth of Venus, The, 33
birthplace, Shakespeare's, 4, *4*
Blackfriars Theatre, 60
blank verse, 15
Bleak Mid-Winter, In the, 54
"blocking", 42
Boleyn, Anne, 54, 60
box office, 13
Branagh, Kenneth, 46, 54
Brook, Peter, 54
Bullen, Anne, 54, 60
Burbage, Richard, 10, *10,* 11, 54, 60

"calling", 42
Campion, Edmund, 6, *6*
Cardenio, 60
Carey, George, Lord Hunsdon, 54, 55
Carey, Henry, Lord Hunsdon, 54
casting, 42, 43
catharsis, 56
Catholicism, 6, 37, 54, 56, 60
Chain of Being, 6, *6,* 28, 56
Chamberlain's Men, 10, 11, 12, 13, 54, 55, 60
Changeling, The, 55
character, 22, 23, 30, 34, 35
Charles II, 38
Chimes at Midnight, 55
Christianity, 6, 25, 37, 54, 56, 60
Civil War, English, 11, 13, 56
clowns, 11, 33, 56
Coleridge, Samuel Taylor, 39, 54
comedies, 3, 14, 22-27, 33, 56
    early, 22
    happy, 22-23
    problem plays, 16, 22, 24-25, 56
    romances, 22, 26-27, 31, 56
Comedy of Errors, The, 22, *22,* 48, 60
comic scenes, 21, *21*
Condell, Henry, 54
Coriolanus, 16, 20, *20,* 48, 60
corruption, 24, 25
costume design, 42, 43, 44, *44*

costumes, 11, *11,* 12, 39, 40, *40,* 41, 42, 43, 44, *44,* 45
critics, 18, 54, 56
Cromwell, Oliver, 56
Cupid, 37, *37*
Curtain Theatre, 60
Cymbeline, 16, 22, 26, 27, 36, *36,* 48, 60

dance, 23, *23,* 26
"dark lady", the, 32
dates of Shakespeare's works, 3, 16, 22, 28, 60
Davenant, William, 38
Death of Ophelia, The, 46
Dench, Judi, 39, 54
designers, 42, 43, 44
designs,
    costume, 42, 43, 44, *44*
    set, 40, 42, 43
directing styles, 18, 40-41
directors, 40, 41, 42, 43, 45, 56
Donne, John, 54
drama
    Elizabethan, 14-15
    Greek, 54, 56
    in Shakespeare's England, 14-15
    Jacobean, 14, 15
dress rehearsals, 42, 45
Dr Faustus, 14, *14,* 55
Dryden, John, 54
Duchess of Malfi, The, 14, *14,* 55

Edward II, 55
Edward III, *28*
Elizabeth I, 6, 7, 10, 54, 60
Elizabethan beliefs, 6-7
Elizabethan period, 6-15, 56
    drama in, 14-15
    London in, 8-9
    theatre in, 10-13, 38, 39
endings, 17, 23, 24, 26, 27
Every Man in His Humour, 60
excommunication, 56, 60
exile, 56

fair copies, 15, *15,* 56
fairies, 2, *2,* 7, *7,* 22, *22,* 33
fairy-tale plots, 22, 24, 27
families, 26, 27
farce, 56
fatal flaw, 56
fate, 17
feminism, 36, 41, 56
figures of speech, 34, 56
film productions, 46, 54, 55
First Folio, 2, *2,* 15, *15,* 33, 54, 56, 60
Fletcher, John, 3, 54
fools, 22, 56
foot (in poetry), 15, 56
foul papers, 15, *15,* 56

Game at Chess, A, 55
Garrick, David, 38, *38,* 54
"gatherers", 13
ghosts, 18, *18,* 37
Gielgud, John, 39, *39,* 54
Globe Theatre, 12-13, *12-13,* 55, 60
    rebuilding of, 13, *13,* 55
gods, 27, 37
good quartos, 56
Greek drama, 54, 56
Greek gods, 37
Greek myths, 26
Greenaway, Peter, 54
groundlings, 12

Hall, Edward, 29
hamartia, 56
Hamlet, 3, *3,* 6, 7, *7,* 16, *16,* 18, *18,* 19, *19,* 39, *39,* 42, *42,* 46, *46,* 47, 49, 54, 55, 60
Hathaway, Anne, 4, 5, 60
'heavens", 12
Heminge, John, 54
Henry IV, 28, *28*
Henry IV, Part I, 28, 29, 30, 31, *31,* 35, *35,* 49, 54, 55, 60
Henry IV, Part II, 28, 29, 30, 31, 49, 54, 55, 60
Henry V, 3, 11, 13, 28, 29, 30, 31, 46, 49, 54, 55, 60
Henry VI, 28, *28,* 29
Henry VI, Part I, 28, 29, 49, 60
Henry VI, Part II, 28, 29, 49, 60
Henry VI, Part III, 28, 29, 49, 60
Henry VII, 28, 29
Henry VIII, 28, *28,* 29, 54, 60
Henry VIII, 13, 28, 31, 50, 54, 60
Herbert, William, 33
history plays, 3, 14, 16, 28-31, 54, 56
    earlier, 28-29
    later, 30-31
Holinshed, Raphael, 54
Holy Trinity Church, Stratford, 5, *5,* 60
Hugo, François Victor, 54
humours, 7, 56
Hunsdon, Lord, *see* Carey
hyperbole, 34

iambic foot, 15, 56
iambic pentameters, 15, 56
idioms, 35
imagery, 32, 34, 35, 56
innuendo, 22, 23
insanity, 19
interpretation, 3, 40, 41
Irving, Henry, 39, 54, 55

Jacobean period, 14, 15, 56
James I of England and VI of Scotland, 10, 14, 55, 60
jesters, 22, 56
Jews, 37, 40, 56
jig, 56
Johnson, Samuel, 54, 55
jokes, 22, 23
Jonson, Ben, 14, *14,* 55, 60
Julius Caesar, 20, *20*
Julius Caesar, 3, *3,* 7, 16, 20, 21, *21,* 50, 60
justice, 25

Kean, Edmund, 39, *39,* 55
Kempe, Will, 11, *11,* 55
King Edward VI Grammar School, 5, *5*
King John, 31, *31*
King John, 28, 31, 50, 60
King Lear, 15, *15,* 16, 18, 19, *19,* 38, 39, *42,* 44, 46, 50, 54, 55, 60
King's Men, 10, 55, 60
kingship, 28, 29, 30, 31
Kurosawa, Akira, 46, 55
Kyd, Thomas, 14

Lamb, Charles and Mary, 55
Lancaster, House of, 28, 29, 56
language in Shakespeare's plays, 3, 20, 21, 32, 33, 34-35
law, 25
Leicester's Men, 10, 60
Lennox, Charlotte, 55
lighting, 40, 42, 44, 45
line references, 3

literary criticism, 54, 56
London, 4, 5, 8-9, *8-9*, 10, 11, 12, 13, *13*, 14,
    60
    City of, 8, 10
love, 20, 22, 23, 24, 26, 27, 32, 33, 36, 37
Lover's Complaint, The, 33
Love's Labour's Lost, 22, 50, 60
Love's Labour's Won, 60
Luther, Martin, 56

Macbeth, 15, *15*, 16, *16*, 17, *17*, 18, 19, *19*, 21,
    21, 35, *35*, 36, *36*, 39, *39*, 46, 47, 50, 54,
    55, 60
magic, 7, 22, 24, 26, 27, 37
make-up, 45, *45*
Malone, Edmond, 55
Marlowe, Christopher, 14, 55, 60
marriage, 5, 23, 24, 25, 33, 36, 41
Mary Queen of Scots, 60
masques, 26, *26*, 56
Measure for Measure, 22, 24, 25, *25*, 40, 51, 60
medicine, 6, *6*
medieval period, 56
melancholy, 7, 23
Merchant of Venice, The, 15, 22, 23, 36, 37, 40,
    40, 51, 60
mercy, 25, 27
Merry Wives of Windsor, The, 22, 44, *44*, 51,
    54, 60
metaphors, 32, 34, 35, 56
Middle Ages, 6, 56
Middleton, Thomas, 55
Midsummer Night's Dream, A, 2, *2*, 7, *7*, 10,
    10, 22, *22*, 39, *39*, 43, *43*, 51, 54, 60
modern-dress productions, 39, *39*, 40, *40*
morality plays, 14, 56
Much Ado About Nothing, 22, 23, *23*, 38, *38*,
    46, 51, 54, 60
musicals, 47
mystery plays, 14, 56
myths, 26

nature, 27, 32
New Place, 5, *5*, 60

"off book", 42, 44
Olivier, Laurence, 39, 46, 55
operas, 47
oracles, 56
Otello, 47, *47*
Othello, 16, 18, *18*, 36, 39, *39*, 46, 47, 51, 54,
    55, 60

paganism, 37, 56
pastoral, 56
pathos, 56
patrons, 10, 32, 33, *33*, 54, 55, 56
performing Shakespeare, 3, 38, 39, 40-45
Pericles, 22, 26, 27, 52, 60
Philaster, 54
Phoenix and the Turtle, The, 33
plague, 8, *8*, 11, 56, 60
players, 11
plots, 15, 22, 23, 48-53, 56
Poel, William, 55
Poetics, The, 54
poetry, 15, 32-33, 54
printers, 15
problem plays, 16, 22, 24-25, 56
productions, 3, 38, 39, 40-45
    film, 46, 54, 55
    modern-dress, 39, *39*, 40, *40*
    television, 46
    touring, 42, 43
prophecies, 17, 56

props, 12, 40, 41, 42, 44, 56
prose, 15
protagonists, 16, 56
Protestantism, 6, 37, 54, 56
Puritans, 6, 11, 13, 38, 56

quartos, 15, *15*, 56
Queen's Men, 60

race and racial prejudice, 18, 36, 37, 40
Ran, 46, *46*, 55
Rape of Lucrece, The, 33, 55, 60
Reduced Shakespeare Company, 47, *47*
Reformation, 6, 56
rehearsals, 11, 15, 42, *42*, 43, 44, 45
    dress, 42, 45
    technical, 42, 44
religion, 6, 7, 25, 37, 54, 56, 60
Renaissance, 56
Restoration, 11, 38, 56
Restoration Shakespeare, 38, *38*, 54
Return to the Forbidden Planet, 47
rhetoric, 21, 56
rhyme schemes, 32, 56
rhyming couplets, 32, 56
rhythm, 15, 35
Richard II, 28, *28*
Richard II, 28, 29, 30, *30*, 35, *35*, 52, 60
Richard III, 29, *29*
Richard III, 28, 29, *29*, 52, 55, 60
Roman gods, 37
Roman tragedies, 20-21
romances, 22, 26-27, 31, 56
Romeo and Juliet, 16, 17, *17*, 40, *40*, 46, 47,
    52, 55, 60
Rose Theatre, 10, *10*, 60
Rosencrantz and Guildenstern are Dead, 47
Rowe, Nicholas, 55
Royal Shakespeare Company, 5

St. Paul's Cathedral, 8
satire, 14, 56
scenery, 11, 12, 38, 39
scenes, 3, 56
Schelling, Karoline, 55
Schlegel, August Wilhelm von, 55
school, Shakespeare's, 5, *5*
set design, 40, 42, 43
sets, 40, 42, 43, *43*, 44, 45, 56
"shadow", 12
Shakespeare, Hamnet, 4, 60
Shakespeare, John, 4, 60
Shakespeare, Judith, 4, 60
Shakespeare, Susanna, 4, 5, 60
Shakespeare Jubilee, 38, 54
Siddons, Sarah, 55
Sidney, Philip, 32
similes, 34, 35, 56
Sir Thomas More, 15, *15*
slapstick, 22
Sly, William, 11
soliloquies, 16
songs, 22, 23, 26, 33
sonnet sequences, 32
sonnets, 3, 32, *32*, 33, 55, 56, 60
sound effects, 11, 40
Southampton, Earl of, *see* Wriothesley, Henry
Spanish Armada, 60
Spanish Tragedy, The, 14
special effects, 11, 26, 44
stage,
    apron, 12, 13, 56
    revolving, 44
Stoppard, Tom, 47
Stratford-upon-Avon, 4-5, *4-5*, 38, 54, 60

subplots, 56
supernatural beliefs, 7, 37
supernatural characters and events, 7, 17, 18,
    26, 27, 37
Swan Theatre, 10, *10*, 60

Tales from Shakespeare, 55
Tamburlaine, 14, 55
Taming of the Shrew, The, 22, 36, 41, *41*, 46,
    52, 55, 60
Tate, Nahum, 38, 39
technical rehearsal or "tech", 42, 44
television productions, 46
Tempest, The, 2, *2*, 13, 22, 26, *26*, 27, *27*, 33,
    43, *43*, 44, *44*, 47, 52, 54, 60
Terry, Ellen, 39, *39*, 54, 55
The Theatre, 10, 13, 60
theatre companies, 5, 10, 11, 42, 45
    Chamberlain's Men, 10, 11, 12, 13, 54, 55,
        60
    King's Men, 10, 55, 60
    Leicester's Men, 10, 60
    Queen's Men, 60
theatres, 10-13
    Blackfriars, 60
    The Curtain, 60
    The Globe, 12-13, *12-13*, 55, 60
    The Rose, 10, *10*, 60
    The Swan, 10, *10*, 60
    The Theatre, 10, 13, 60
Throne of Blood, 46, 55
Timon of Athens, 16, 53, 55, 60
Titus Andronicus, 14, 16, 17, *17*, 53, 60
touring productions, 42, 43
tragedies, 3, 14, 16-21, 23, 56
    early, 17
    great, 18-19, 30
    revenge, 14, 17
    Roman, 20-21
tragicomedies, 14, 23, 56
translation of Shakespeare's works, 39, 54, 55
Tree, Herbert Beerbohm, 39, 55
Troilus and Cressida, 16, 22, 24, *24*, 53, 54, 60
Tudor, House of, 28, 29
Twelfth Night, 11, *11*, 22, 23, 33, *33*, 46, *46*,
    53, 60
Two Gentlemen of Verona, The, 22, 53, 60
Two Noble Kinsmen, The, 22, 53, 54, 60

understudies, 43, 45

Venus and Adonis, 33, 55, 60
Verdi, Guiseppe, 47
Volpone, 14, *14*

W. H., Mr, 32, 33
Wanamaker, Sam, 13, 55
Wars of the Roses, 28, 29, *29*, 56
Webster, John, 14, 55
weddings, *see* marriage
Welles, Orson, 55
West Side Story, 47, *47*
White Devil, The, 55
Winter's Tale, The, 14, 22, 26, 27, 37, *37*, 53,
    60
witches, 7, *7*, 17, *17*, 18, 37
Women Beware Women, 55
women's roles, 11, 23, 36
Wriothesley, Henry, Earl of Southampton,
    32, *32*, 33, *33*, 55

York, House of, 28, 29, 56

Zeffirelli, Franco, 46, 55
zodiac, 7, *7*

Acknowledgements

The publishers are grateful to the following for their permission to reproduce material:
Cover: Ian Holm as King Lear, ©Donald Cooper/Photostage.
2-3: *A Midsummer Night's Dream*, ©Donald Cooper/Photostage; *Hamlet*, ©Henrietta Butler/Performing Arts Library; Droeshout engraving of Shakespeare, Bodleian Library Arch.Gc.8.; *The Tempest* and *Julius Caesar* pictures taken from First Folio Postcards by ©Louisa Hare and reprinted by kind permission of Louisa Hare. Protected by copyright.
4-5: Shakespeare's birthplace, King Edward VI School and Holy Trinity Church, ©Jarrold Publishing and reproduced by kind permission of the Shakespeare Birthplace Trust, King Edward VI School and Holy Trinity Church. Thanks to the Shakespeare Birthplace Trust for permission to use their map of Stratford as a reference. The original map is on display at the exhibition "Shakespeare: His Life and Background" at the Shakespeare's Birthplace Visitors' Centre, Stratford-upon-Avon.
6-7: Medical instruments, ©Science & Society Picture Library/Science Museum; Campion on rack, Mansell Collection; Toyah Wilcox as Puck, ©Fritz Curzon/Performing Arts Library; Kenneth Branagh as Hamlet, ©Donald Cooper/Photostage; Witch hanging woodcut, the Shakespeare Centre Library: Stratford-upon-Avon.
8-9: Cockfighting pit, reproduced by kind permission of Edinburgh University Library; View of London by Visscher (detail), Mansell Collection; Plague skeleton (title page from Dekker's *A Rod for Run-aways*), Bodleian Library Mal.601 (1).
10-11: Richard Burbage self-portrait, reproduced by kind permission of the trustees of Dulwich Picture Gallery; Rose Theatre stamp, reproduced by kind permission of Royal Mail; Wall scene from *A Midsummer Night's Dream*, ©Donald Cooper/Photostage; Viola/Cesario in *Twelfth Night*, Raymond Mander and Joe Mitchenson Theatre Collection/Angus McBean; Swan Theatre drawing, University Library, Utrecht, MS 842, f. 132r; Will Kempe, Fotomas Index.
12-13: The Globe from a view of London by Visscher, Mansell Collection; New Shakespeare's Globe under construction, ©Richard Kalina, with thanks to the Globe Education Centre.
14-15: *Volpone*, Raymond Mander and Joe Mitchenson Theatre Collection; Dr Faustus from title page of 1631 edition, Bodleian Library Mal.210 (1); Juliet Stevenson as Duchess of Malfi, ©Donald Cooper/Photostage; Alan Howard as Macbeth, ©John Haynes, with thanks to Nicola Scadding and the National Theatre, London; Page from the manuscript of *Sir Thomas More*, By permission of the British Library (Harl.7368 folio 9); Title page of Quarto of *King Lear*, Bodleian Library Arch.Gd.42; "Principall Actors" page from First Folio, Bodleian Library Arch.Gc.7.
16-17: Hamlet caricature, Raymond Mander and Joe Mitchenson Theatre Collection; *Titus Andronicus*, Copyright ©BBC; *Romeo and Juliet* balcony scene, Raymond Mander and Joe Mitchenson Theatre Collection/Angus McBean;

Three witches, the Shakespeare Centre Library: Stratford-upon-Avon.
18-19: Ghost in *Hamlet*, Theatre Museum, V&A; *Othello*, Raymond Mander and Joe Mitchenson Theatre Collection; Warren Mitchell as King Lear and Trevor Baxter as Gloucester, ©Donald Cooper/Photostage; Ophelia, the Shakespeare Centre Library: Stratford-upon-Avon; Macbeth, picture taken from First Folio Postcards by ©Louisa Hare and reprinted by kind permission of Louisa Hare. Protected by copyright.
20-21: Toby Stephens as Coriolanus, ©Henrietta Butler/Performing Arts Library; *Antony and Cleopatra*, Raymond Mander and Joe Mitchenson Theatre Collection; *Julius Caesar*, Keith Michell as Antony, Copyright ©BBC; *Macbeth* porter scene, Raymond Mander and Joe Mitchenson Theatre Collection.
22-23: *The Comedy of Errors*, picture taken from First Folio Postcards by ©Louisa Hare and reprinted by kind permission of Louisa Hare. Protected by copyright. *A Midsummer Night's Dream*, Maggie Smith as Titania, Zoe Dominic/©Dominic Photography; Sinead Cusack as Beatrice and Derek Jacobi as Benedick, ©Donald Cooper/Photostage; Peggy Ashcroft as Beatrice and John Gielgud as Benedick, Raymond Mander and Joe Mitchenson Theatre Collection; *Much Ado About Nothing* dance scene, Zoe Dominic/©Dominic Photography; Alan Rickman as Jaques, ©Donald Cooper/Photostage.
24-25: Sophie Thompson as Helena, Toby Stephens as Bertram and Barbara Jefford as the Countess in *All's Well That Ends Well*, ©Donald Cooper/Photostage; *Measure for Measure* with Stella Gonet as Isabella, ©Henrietta Butler/Performing Arts Library; *Troilus and Cressida* picture taken from First Folio Postcards by ©Louisa Hare and reprinted by kind permission of Louisa Hare. Protected by copyright.
26-27: *The Tempest* masque scene, Raymond Mander and Joe Mitchenson Theatre Collection/Angus McBean; Derek Jacobi as Prospero, ©Donald Cooper/Photostage; Warren Clarke as Caliban, Copyright ©BBC; Storm scene (title page from 1709 edition of *The Tempest*), Fotomas Index.
28-29: Ron Cook as Richard III, Copyright ©BBC.
30-31: Derek Jacobi as Richard II, Copyright ©BBC; Fiona Shaw as Richard II, ©Neil Libbert, with thanks to Nicola Scadding and the National Theatre, London; Anthony Quayle as Falstaff, Copyright ©BBC; Anthony Quayle as Falstaff and Brenda Bruce as Hostess in *Henry IV* tavern scene, Copyright ©BBC.
32-33: Title page of Shakespeare's sonnets, Bodleian Library Arch.Gd.41 (2); Portrait of Henry Wriothesley, after John de Critz the Elder, from the Duke of Buccleuch's collection at Boughton House, Northamptonshire; *The Birth of Venus* by Botticelli (detail), ET Archive/Uffizi Gallery Florence; Feste in *Twelfth Night*, ©Donald Cooper/Photostage.

34-35: Anthony Hopkins as Antony and Judi Dench as Cleopatra, ©Donald Cooper/Photostage; Derek Jacobi as Macbeth, ©Donald Cooper/Photostage.
36-37: Geraldine James as Imogen in *Cymbeline*, ©John Haynes, with thanks to Nicola Scadding and the National Theatre, London; Vanessa Redgrave as Rosalind in *As You Like It*, Raymond Mander and Joe Mitchenson Theatre Collection; *Macbeth*, ©Clive Barda/Performing Arts Library; *The Winter's Tale* statue scene, ©Donald Cooper/Photostage; Cupid, picture taken from First Folio Postcards by ©Louisa Hare and reprinted by kind permission of Louisa Hare. Protected by copyright.
38-39: Thomas Betterton portrait, Edmund Kean as Othello, and Ellen Terry as Lady Macbeth, the Shakespeare Centre Library: Stratford-upon-Avon; David Garrick as Benedick, ET Archive/Theatre Museum; John Gielgud as Hamlet, Theatre Museum, V&A; *A Midsummer Night's Dream* (pink umbrella) ©Clive Barda/Performing Arts Library.
40-41: *Romeo and Juliet*, ©Ben Christopher/Performing Arts Library; Frank Benson as Shylock, Raymond Mander and Joe Mitchenson Theatre Collection; Dustin Hoffman as Shylock, Richard H Smith/©Dominic Photography; Josie Lawrence as Katherine, both pics ©Donald Cooper/Photostage.
42-43: Rehearsal of *Hamlet*, ©Donald Cooper/Photostage; *A Midsummer Night's Dream* set, *The Tempest* set, the Shakespeare Centre Library: Stratford-upon-Avon.
44-45: Costume design for Prospero by ©Maria Bjornson, reproduced by kind permission of Maria Bjornson, with thanks to Judy Daish Associates/the Shakespeare Centre Library: Stratford-upon-Avon; Theatrical embroiderer, ©Stuart Franklin/Magnum photos; Latex belly fitting, Make-up room, and Eye make-up, all ©Clive Barda/Performing Arts Library; Half-made-up face, ©Mike Prior.
46-47: *The Death of Ophelia* by John Everett Millais, Tate Gallery London 1996/Photo: John Webb; Poster for Akiro Kurosawa's *Ran*, BFI; Malvolio from Animated Tales from Shakespeare (*Twelfth Night*), Copyright ©BBC; The Reduced Shakespeare Company, ©Stephen Sweet, with thanks to The Reduced Shakespeare Company and Duff Publicity; Placido Domingo as Otello in Verdi's *Otello*, ©Clive Barda/Performing Arts Library; *West Side Story* ©Donald Cooper/Photostage.

Every effort has been made to trace copyright holders of material in this book. If any rights have been omitted, the publishers offer their apologies and will rectify this in any subsequent editions following notification.

Editorial and picture assistant: Rachael Swann.
Photography on pages 42-45 by Howard Allman.
Consultant: Julia Briggs.
Quotations are taken from the Oxford Shakespeare, ed. Stanley Wells and Gary Taylor; OUP 1988.